You Are Free

realise your true nature to be happy

RANJIT NATH

Cover Design and Illustration:
Ashutosh Nimbreart

INDIA • SINGAPORE • MALAYSIA

ISBN 979-8-89186-881-6

Dedicated to all children

Contents

Introduction

It is a common belief, across the world, that school education doesn't prepare us for the realities of life. As I am experiencing my own life and going through the ups and downs, I also reflect on this issue. Is my school education helping me to live a good life? Was I prepared to face my life, the way I am experiencing it now?

After completing my education, I got a good job due to my college qualifications and achieved many things in life. I got busy with job responsibilities, career growth, family, raising kids, buying houses, changing cars, and going on holidays. Hardly I had any time to think beyond these boundaries of life.

In the last 50 years, as I am steering my life through the already laid down boundaries, I have experienced many happy moments fulfilling my desires in my job, family, and personally. There were equally challenging times that left me unhappy, sad, angry, and disappointed.

At this time of my life, when I am reflecting on my life with a fresh perspective, many questions come to my mind. The chief among them is thinking about what is the purpose of my life. What am I supposed to do next? Am I supposed to complete the remaining years of my life just by doing things that come to me and moving on?

That will mean I am just waiting to die without any purpose.

I hear many retired people saying that they are doing something just to pass the time or earn some money. This gives me the feeling that after retirement from the job, there is no real purpose left in life. Does it mean they have achieved the purpose of their life completing their professional career and fulfilling their family responsibilities?

Is life just a simple sum of career and family and friends? Even if I add some community service or similar work that we consider meaningful and satisfactory, can I say I have met the purpose of my life? Am I really happy with what I have done in my life so far?

I don't get an easy answer. Instead, all these questions leave me with some kind of uneasy empty feeling inside. And I don't think another promotion in the job, one more house or a bigger car, or even some community service is going to fill this emptiness within me.

What is it that I want then? School education did not teach me this. Neither have I learned about it in many training sessions that I have attended in my professional life. I need to find the answer myself.

As I am juggling these thoughts and going through this phase of my life, I face another challenge. I am supposed to guide my two daughters in their life. They are growing up fast and I feel responsible for teaching them something about life. When I have my own doubts about my life, how do I guide my children in their lives? If I do that, will that be honest? This could be a problem for many.

With these thoughts, I started to explore to find an answer.

When I read Daniel Goleman's book about Emotional Intelligence and learned that childhood represents a special window of opportunity for emotional lessons, I was convinced that this is probably the most important thing a child should learn in school. There is no doubt that an Emotionally Intelligent child can face life better and do well in his or her life than just someone with only a higher IQ. There are many initiatives to improve the EQ of children. Many Universities and organisations are researching and teaching Emotional Intelligence at schools and colleges.

I continued my journey of exploring more. I came across an excellent course on Positive Psychology by Prof. Martin Seligman on Coursera. He is the Director of Penn Positive Psychology Center and was the President of the American Psychology Association in 1998. He has developed a model called PERMA (Positive Emotion, Engagement, Relationships, Meaning and Accomplishments) as a framework to achieve Well-being in life. He also worked extensively to incorporate the PERMA model and Well-being into traditional education and came up with the concept of Positive Education. Martin Seligman and

Christopher Peterson studied the time-tested virtues and characters across the world and defined the "Values In Action" (VIA) classification. The PERMA model of Well-being and VIA Character strengths are taught in some schools as part of Positive Education. This initiative can definitely cover some gaps in school education in preparing a child for life. Achieving Well-being, a well-researched concept covering what one aspires for in life is the goal of Positive Education.

There are many other Psychologists across the world who have developed different psychological tools to help mankind with the psychological challenges they face in life. I was reading the book *"The Resilience Factor"* by Andrew Shatte and Karen Reivich at the time when Cafe Coffee Day owner VG Siddhartha died. When I read his story and learned about the circumstances leading to his death, the first thought that came to my mind was, could this book have made a difference in his life? Could resilience skills have saved his life?

Steve Jobs is a role model example of how passion drives performance. He once said, "People with Passion can change the world". There are many students passionate about something or other in their life. But do all of them perform like what Steve Jobs did? Psychologist Angela Duckworth has an answer to this. Only passion is not enough. Passion and Perseverance, which she called "grit", is the secret of success. She has recommendations on how a child can develop grit.

These are just a few examples of what is available in academia and adopted by some fraction of people across the world. Take any challenging area of life, there will be research and tools to handle such challenges. However, not all such solutions reach those who really need them. Assuming many of these methods are taught at school to students to prepare them for the future, the question still remains, "*Is that enough to prepare us for future life?* "

Spending a lot of time reading these books and learning different psychological tools that can help in life, I continued my exploration. What else should be taught in schools to prepare a child better for life?

Being in India, we are exposed to spirituality from childhood. Visiting temples with parents, celebrating different religious festivals, and listening to and participating in religious discussions bring spiritual awareness to us. Even though not fully active, spirituality always remains in the back of our minds. Thinking and praying to God, particularly when in a problem, almost happens naturally to us.

Incidentally, I came across a social media post of Indian Cricket Captain Virat Kohli holding the book "Autobiography of a Yogi" by Paramahansa Yogananda. Kohli wrote on Instagram, *"I love this book. A must-read for all those who are brave enough to let their thoughts and ideologies be challenged. The understanding and implementation of the knowledge in this book will change your whole perspective and life. Believe in the divine and keep marching on doing good deeds #onelove #begrateful #helponeanother"*

In the last few years, this book has brought a significant change to my life. After reading this book, I read many other spiritual books including Bhagavad Gita by Paramahansa Yogananda, and learned about Jnana Yoga and Karma Yoga from the writing of Vivekananda, Patanjali Yoga Sutras by SriSwami Satchidananda, and so on. I also started learning meditation seriously and started practising it.

This has changed my outlook on spirituality and what spirituality can do to our lives.

I was of the opinion that Spirituality and Science have conflicting views. So, while reading spirituality, I was also exploring science to understand the scientific view of creation. I read Stephen Hawking's *"The Grand Design"* and a few other similar books about how this universe has come into existence. To be honest, it was hard for me to understand the technical details of the unanswered questions about the creation of the universe, but I could get a clear idea of the challenge that science is facing to explain how we came into existence. We are still far from knowing the Universe and its origin.

In contrast, Spirituality gives a clear explanation of the creation. Spirituality seems to have answers to those questions that science has not been able to comprehend till now. The consistency and clarity with what spirituality explains our origin, compared to what science is able to do till now, makes me believe that spirituality has more sophisticated tools of learning than what science uses. Unless someone has discovered such deep knowledge, it cannot come from imagination or without any scientific basis.

We all know the Late APJ Kalam as the "Missile Man of India" and as the most popular and visionary President. I did not know much about his Spiritual view till the time I read his book *"Transcendence - My Spiritual Experience with Pramukh Swamiji"*. After reading this book by one of the greatest scientists in our nation, I started realising the harmony and differences between Science and Spirituality. The realm of Science and the realm of Spirituality are different, but they are complementary, not conflicting.

After exploring for many years what else a child should learn early in life to face life better, I found two options - Positive Psychology and Spirituality. Both can bring positive change to our lives. But if I need to choose one among them to learn, which one should I pick first? I was in that dilemma for some time. When I thought deeply about it, it became obvious to me. As far as Psychology is concerned, the definition of life starts at birth and ends with death. However, spirituality believes life is eternal. Psychology can help us in the short term, but spirituality will help us in the long term of our lives. I realised that spirituality gives us a more holistic solution.

With this background, I came to the conclusion that if we want to make our lives better, Spirituality needs to be an integral part of our lives, not just an occasional reading or practice.

Spirituality and only Spirituality have the answer to fill that emptiness or void that we feel within us at some point in our lives. Nothing else in this material world can compensate for that. It is not because the things in the world are not good enough. It is because of our nature. Our real nature is such that only by practising spirituality we can achieve real fulfilment. Material achievement can give us only momentary pleasure, not real happiness.

If we want happiness and completeness in our lives, we need to learn and practice spirituality and start it early in life. Schools should teach spirituality and practice of spirituality to students as part of their curriculum to prepare them for life, in a similar way to what earlier *gurukuls* used to do in India.

There is a difference between Spiritual truths and religious practices that we generally see in our day-to-day lives. What we see are the rituals and mythological stories of different religions. The spiritual truths or the knowledge found in religion are much deeper than the practices. They are the truths of our life. When I am talking about spirituality, I am referring to this knowledge. This knowledge and correct practice of spirituality can make our lives better.

Spiritual books that I have read are written for an adult audience. I have a habit of discussing my new learning with my 13-year-old daughter. Her innocent but deep questions motivate me to share more with her. This is when I realised that these books are not suitable for them to read directly. Most of the spiritual books available for children are generally mythology stories. But the actual spiritual knowledge is much deeper than that.

If the Bhagavad Gita teaches us how to live a good life, then why not a child learn this divine knowledge early in their life?

I felt there is a need to present this sea of divine knowledge about our lives in a simpler and comprehensible way so that a child can appreciate it early in life. This is the motivation for writing this book.

My exploration started when I started thinking about what was next in my life. This forced me to ask the fundamental question about the purpose and meaning of my life. Whenever I tried to find an answer to this question, I felt some uneasy emptiness within me, in spite of having a comfortable life with good financial security and a happy family around me. What can fulfil that emptiness within me? What should be the priorities of my life? This problem was magnified when I realised that as a father, I am supposed to guide my two daughters in their life. Having doubts about my own life, what advice can I give to them? Will it be honest if I suggest something to them but I myself am not convinced about that.

Finally, I have found the answer in spirituality. This is what I want to tell my daughter and the younger generation through this book.

To keep the emotion alive, I have written the book as a conversation between me and my daughter, trying to give a genuine answer to a fundamental question any child can ask, *"What should I do when I grow up?"*.

As I have explained before, it is not my answer. I am too small to find this answer myself. The answer is already in the knowledge of spirituality. My effort is to show this answer to the child in a way so that he or she can appreciate it and hopefully adopt it in their life early. I hope this book will equip parents to give a more genuine and truthful answer when they face this question.

Though the book is targeted at younger kids, my recommendation is that the parent should read the book together with the child. In spite of trying my best, some content might be difficult for a young child to understand alone. Omitting those contents will not convey the complete information.

This book also has the answer to my own question about what is the purpose of my life. How do I decide the priorities of my life? Why do I feel that emptiness within me and what can satisfy that? There could be many more like me who might have faced the same question in life or might have felt that emptiness within them in spite of having many other accomplishments in life. This book is for those adults.

* * *

Acknowledgement

My younger daughter Manasvi (fondly called Manu) is my primary source of inspiration for writing this book. Our small small conversations about spirituality at home and her innocent but profound questions about different spiritual facts have inspired me to learn more and tell more to her. I am wholeheartedly grateful to her for actively participating in this journey alongside me. Without her, I would not have written this book.

Illustrating the abstract concepts in this book posed a considerable challenge demanding multiple discussions and exploring many ideas. I sincerely extend my heartfelt thanks to Ashutosh Nimbreart for skillfully illustrating my book. The cover design and illustrations would not have been possible without the support of my elder daughter Anisha, who validated all my ideas and improvised them.

Busy with my office responsibilities most of the time, I had to use my personal time to write this book. There were times when I could not give enough time to my family during the weekends. I am grateful to my wife Gitanjali for her unwavering support in providing an environment where I could complete my work.

Tea breaks and small walks at the workplace with like-minded friends are a happy hunting ground for many new ideas. Taking a break from work, we often discuss our life, philosophy, interests, family, and many other things during these break times. This book is an outcome of such discussions with some of my friends at my workplace, where the seed of doing something new was put in my mind and germinated over many years receiving nourishment from different life experiences. I am grateful to all my friends with whom I had such deep discussions about people and life who have influenced this book directly or indirectly.

Finally, I express my gratitude to all my friends and well-wishers who have taken the time to read the manuscript and offered their invaluable suggestions, aiding me in refining and enhancing the content. Your support has been truly appreciated.

• 1 •

Purpose of Life

Manu: Papa, I just completed reading the book "Wings of Fire" by Abdul Kalam.

Papa: Oh! Very good. Did you like the book?

Manu: Yes. I liked the book. It is a very nice book. But I have a question.

Papa: What is your question?

Manu: In the book, I read that Abdul Kalam first wanted to become an Air Force Pilot. He wanted to fly. But actually, he became one of the greatest scientists. And then later he became our President also.

Papa: Yes. I also read about him. Kalam was highly dejected after he failed to clear the Air Force Selection Board interview. In fact, he was very close to getting the job as he stood ninth in the rank, but unfortunately, there were only eight positions. So, he did not qualify.

Manu: He was very disappointed. But then later, as a scientist, he was very successful. He was one of the most popular Presidents of India.

Papa: He is also known as the *"Missile Man of India"* for his contribution to space research. So, what is your question?

Manu: What should I do when I grow up?

Papa: Good, you are thinking about it. What do you want to become?

Manu: I am not very sure. When I read my science book, sometimes I think I should become a scientist and invent something new. Sometimes I also think I should become a teacher. I really don't know what I want to become when I grow up. But I definitely want to become a pianist. I also like dancing, though sometimes I feel my interest is reducing.

Papa: You have many options. And as you grow up, maybe your interest will change and you will become a doctor or take up some other profession. Who knows.

Manu: So how to decide what I will do? Is it based on my interest? But if I have more than one interest?

Papa: Let me ask you a question. What do you want in your life?

Manu: Let me think!! I think I want a big house, a nice car and money to go to some nice places around the world. I want to keep many pets in my house. Of course, I want to be happy.

Papa: That should not be a big problem. You know how to get them. If you study well, you will be able to get a good job. Once you have a good job, you can have sufficient money to buy a good house, you can go on holiday to nice places and have fun. Most people doing a decent job can achieve that. But you also said you want to be happy. There could be some problems in getting that.

Happiness is not guaranteed in our life.

Manu: Why? If I have a good job and lots of money, why can't I be happy?

Papa: Do you know what gives you happiness?

Manu: Many things give me happiness. When I do well in the exam, I feel good. When you or Ma give me something nice, I feel happy. Our trip to Disneyland in Hong Kong was so much fun. The view of the snow-covered mountains during our Gangtok trip was so beautiful. When I play with my friends, I enjoy it. There are many things that make me happy or feel good.

Papa: Great. Are you always happy?

Manu: Definitely not. There are moments when I am not happy. When I make silly mistakes on math tests, I feel very sad. Sometimes I fight with my friends and I feel bad. When we come back from holiday, I feel sad thinking that the good time is over. When my sister Esha comes home from the hostel, I feel good, but when she leaves, I feel sad. I think there are equally many things that make me sad!!

Papa: Exactly. It is not easy to tell what makes us happy.

As you said, during the holiday you feel good, but when the holiday is over you feel sad. When your sister comes from the hostel you are happy, but when she leaves you feel unhappy. When you play with friends you enjoy it, but when you have a fight with your friend you feel sad. If you do well in the test you are happy, if you don't do well, you are sad.

Manu: True.

Papa: The same thing makes you happy as well as unhappy. Going on vacation makes you both happy and unhappy. Your sister coming back home from the hostel makes you feel good and also makes you feel sad. The company of your friends is enjoyable but not always.

Manu: Why does it happen like that?

Papa: Because of our nature.

Manu: What does that mean?

Papa: I will tell you. Can you tell me what you want from a holiday?

Manu: It's very simple. Lots of fun.

Papa: Going on vacation and having fun during the vacation is what we want. We also don't want it to end. We want to do well in tests, we want to have a good time with our friends, we want nice gifts, and we want our dear ones near us.

These are all our desires.

We have many desires. If our desires are fulfilled, we are happy, if not we are unhappy.

Manu: Then it should be simple. If we know all our desires and work to fulfil them, then we will always be happy. Why do you say happiness is not guaranteed in our life?

Papa: Let's see if it is that simple. Do you know all your desires?

Manu: If I think I should be able to prepare a list.

Papa: It is not simple. In fact, it is impossible.

Do you remember how much you used to like Barbie dolls earlier? But now you don't like them so much. When you got your cycle, you were very excited. But now you don't have the same excitement. You have a smartwatch. You like it, but you prefer a smartphone.

Our desires are not fixed. They keep changing.

Because of our nature, there is no end to our desires. Today we may have a few desires, but tomorrow we will have a few more. Our desires will keep changing and new desires will keep added to the list. We get bored very easily. Our nature is like that. We cannot remain happy with one thing for a long time. We always need something new. Do you like to play the same game all the time?

As you grow up, this problem will get even bigger.

Manu: Why?

Papa: Later you will need a job to earn money so that you can take care of your needs like food, clothes, and health. You will also need a house to stay in.

Once these basic needs are fulfilled, then you will have more requirements. For example, you will need a car. If you buy a small car, after some time you want to buy a big car. If you stay in a small house, you want to buy a bigger house. First, you want to go on holiday to different places in India. Then you want to go to the most exotic places in the world.

Manu: If we can earn more money, we can get more and better things. We will be happier.

Papa: That is how we generally think. But it is not true.

We want more because we want to be happy. But we don't realize that the things that we seek so much cannot make us happy. We think a bigger house, a big car, and a holiday in a nice place will make us happier. We enter a rat race seeking more and more things in life. Our desires keep on increasing and we don't know how to come out of this rat race.

More than that, unfortunately, we don't get the happiness that we want from all these desires.

Manu: Why is it so difficult to control our desires? After we have the necessary things, we can stop desiring more.

Papa: This is human nature. We want happiness and we want happiness to be permanent.

We seek happiness by fulfilling our desires. When a desire is fulfilled, we get some pleasure. After some time, we will get bored with what we got and we will need something new. The happiness that we wanted so much from the fulfilled desire fades away and anxiety to fulfil a new desire occupies our minds. And this process continues.

Manu: What can satisfy us completely then?

Papa: That is a million-dollar question. We will learn that.

Our needs are hierarchical. First, we have Physical needs, then we have Psychological, and finally, we have Spiritual needs.

Actually, the problem is bigger than what I have explained to you just now. Most of the examples we discussed now are physical like a house or car or money. Fulfilling only these physical needs is not enough. We have more needs. For example, we want to help others, we want satisfaction from our work, and we want others to say good things about us. These are examples of psychological desires.

Once our basic physical needs are fulfilled, we have psychological needs. We want good relationships, good quality work, love and care, and recognition. Because of this, even after having a big house, a big car, and a lot of money, we will not be happy because of unfulfilled psychological desires. Only physical things cannot make us happy.

Manu: But is it that difficult to fulfil those psychological desires? If we want, we can do a lot of good work like helping others, and feel good about it. If we do good work others will appreciate us. And if we behave well, don't fight with others, and love others, others will also love us. This is how we can fulfil our psychological desires.

Papa: True. As you are saying, it is possible that we can fulfil many of our psychological needs. It is difficult, but if we try we can achieve that.

Assume we have a good house to live in, we have enough money and a good job. We also have a happy family, everyone loving and caring for each other. All have good health. Assume all our physical and psychological needs are satisfied. Do you think we will be happy?

Manu: I think we should be happy. What else will we need?

Papa: The fact is even after that we will not be satisfied. We will have new desires.

We will start thinking about what's next. What better we can do? We will wonder what is the purpose of this life. We want to understand more about ourselves - the meaning of our life. Why were we born on this earth? What will happen to us after death?

These are called spiritual needs. Once our physical and psychological needs are fulfilled, we will have spiritual needs.

Spiritual needs occur naturally to us and keep us in search of fulfillment.

Manu: That means we can never be happy?

Papa: Don't give up so easily!!

Our entire life we work very hard to fulfil our never-ending list of desires hoping one day we will be happy. But we don't get the happiness for what we work so hard for. We get some momentary pleasure and some miseries too. This happens to almost all people. So, before you jump to decide what you will be doing when you grow up, you should understand why it happens like this.

The world has developed a lot. All luxuries, you name it, are available today. In spite of having many luxuries in life, having good relationships, love and care, receiving good recognition, and good health, still at some point in time in life people wonder what is the purpose of life.

Of course, there are people who struggle to satisfy their basic needs, to have a good job, a good house, good health, or good relationships. But even those who have achieved all these still feel some emptiness within at some point in time of their life.

This means there is something which we don't understand about our life. It is not about what we achieve in life or some shortcoming in the things in the world. It is something about us.

In spite of achieving many things, we still don't feel complete. But we don't know what we are missing.

You can think of our life to be like a jigsaw puzzle game. But a little different from how we normally play. You don't get to see how the final picture will be. And, you have more pieces than what is required to complete the puzzle. Also, there is a small trick. It is mandatory to have one particular piece in the final picture. Without that piece, the puzzle is not complete. And you don't know which is that mandatory piece.

To make it more complex, there is a hidden rule in our life jigsaw puzzle game which is not told to the players. You should use only the optimal number of pieces. It is easier to find the mandatory piece if we use fewer pieces and it becomes more difficult to find that mandatory piece as the number of pieces increases beyond the optimal number.

Manu: I have solved many jigsaw puzzles. But generally, we see the picture of what we are making and we need to use all the puzzle pieces to complete the game. What you are saying is different from that. I could not understand it. Can you help me with some examples?

Papa: Life is simple if we understand it, but very complex if we don't understand it. It is like the jigsaw puzzle example I explained before. When we play the game without understanding, it becomes very hard and complicated. That is what we are doing with our life. But if we understand the game, it becomes simpler. Let me explain with an example.

Good jobs, money, good houses, luxury cars, and relationships are examples of puzzle pieces of the jigsaw puzzle game we are playing in our lives. And happiness is that mandatory piece that is required to complete the puzzle. Everyone wants happiness in life. But we don't know how to get it. We think money will give us happiness. So, we try to earn more money. But later we realize it cannot bring us happiness. So, we search for another piece that can give us happiness. We think good relationships can give us happiness. We try to find good relationships. Again, later we realize it cannot give us real happiness. We search for something else.

Our life is like a jigsaw puzzle game. We think by fulfilling our desires we will get the puzzle pieces to complete our life puzzle and achieve happiness.

Slowly we enter the rat race of desiring more and more things and don't know how to come out of that. Without getting that piece that can give us real happiness, we don't feel complete in our lives. Without realising the hidden rule, we try to get more and more pieces, thus making our life more complex, and don't know how to get that mandatory piece.

Happiness is not just the absence of miseries. It is a continuous state of being in joy. A state of permanent happiness.

If we get every material thing that we wish for in our life, good health and good relationships, at best we will not have any miseries. But that does not mean we are always happy. That is why I said happiness is not guaranteed in our life. We still need to find that missing piece of the life jigsaw puzzle game.

Manu: Has someone solved this life jigsaw puzzle game? Do we know how to find that mandatory piece of happiness to complete the life puzzle?

Papa: Yes, we are going to learn that.

While studying history, you have learned about the invention of the wheel. Imagine the time period before the invention of the wheel. How will people carry things from one place to another place? They will try to drag it on the surface. Are they doing something wrong?

If you know that wheels exist, you will say they are crazy. Why don't they use something with wheels? Then you are wise. But if you don't know that wheels exist, you will find their approach normal. Then you are ignorant. This is an unknown-unknown situation. People did not know what a wheel was and also did not know that something like a wheel could be there. So, they were trying something else.

Our situation is also like that. We don't know what can give us real happiness and we also don't know that there could be something else that can give us real happiness. And we try many other things to get real happiness.

We are ignorant about our ignorance.

Manu: What is our ignorance then?

Papa: If a baby is crying for milk and we give a toy, will the baby stop crying?

We need to know what the baby needs and give that to make the baby stop crying. If we don't know what the baby needs, we will try to give many other things, but that will not quench the thirst of the baby. Our situation is also like a crying baby. We don't know what exactly we want but we know we need something to feel complete.

We don't understand ourselves. We don't know what can make us happy.

We don't know our real nature. This is our ignorance.

Manu: How to know our real nature then?

Papa: It is not a simple answer. Otherwise, we all would have known our real nature. We need to learn about it.

Manu: How to answer my question then? How to decide what I should do when I grow up?

Papa: There are two ways to answer your question.

The first option is very simple. That is what we generally do. We can remain ignorant about our ignorance. I can suggest to you, which profession will have better opportunities and also will match your interest. You will even get many career consulting companies guiding you. If you follow this option, you will collect many pieces of the life jigsaw puzzle game.

But will you find that mandatory piece that can give you happiness? As you collect more and more pieces, you will make your life more and more complicated. Later, at some stage of your life, you will think what am I supposed to do in my life? What is the purpose of my life? You will not get an easy answer. Instead, you will feel some kind of void or emptiness within. And by then you might have already completed a good part of your life. That is not a good situation to be in.

The second option is difficult. We can start to learn what is our real nature and understand what can give us real happiness. If you follow this option, at a later stage of your life, you will not look back and ask yourself if I am doing the right thing in life. By understanding your real nature, you can preempt this question early in your life. You will realize what the most important puzzle pieces you need to solve your life puzzle and how to get that mandatory piece that can give you real happiness.

We can decide on either of these two options. We have free choice to decide.

If we want real happiness in life, then we need to choose the second option. Only by knowing our real nature can we achieve real happiness in life.

Manu: Will you teach me how I can know my real nature?

Papa: If I just tell you what your real nature is, you will not appreciate it.

You need to realize it yourself.

There are methods to realize our true nature. But before that, we need to know some more things. It is very late now. Tomorrow morning you need to go to school and I also need to go to work. Let's sleep now. Tomorrow we will discuss this.

Manu: Oh! It is very late. I will wait for tomorrow evening to discuss more. Good night.

Papa: Good night.

• 2 •

Source of Knowledge

Manu: Yesterday you said I need to know my real nature before I decide what I should do when I grow up. How to know my real nature?

Papa: Yes. We will talk about that. Before that let me ask you a question. What do you know about religion?

Manu: About religion?

I know we are Hindu. And I know Christianity, Islam, Jainism, and Buddhism are some other religions. We have read about religions in our Social Science book.

Papa: What else have you read about religion?

Manu: I have read about Jainism and Buddhism in the chapter "Great Thinkers and New Beliefs" of our Social Science Textbook.

Papa: Can you tell me what you know about Jainism and Buddhism?

Manu: Jainism became popular under Mahavira. When Mahavira was of the age of 30 and was married and had a child, renounced his family to search for the truth.

Mahavira means the great victor who had conquered the self. His main teachings were - absolute non-violence, honesty, kindness, truthfulness and not desiring things belonging to others.

He was also called Jina - one who has conquered anger, passion, greed, and ego through meditation and self-awareness.

Papa: Wow! You have learned many important things about religion.

You have mentioned that Mahavira was searching for the truth. You also said that he conquered the self. Make a note of this. We will learn what are those truths and what conquering the self means. It will help me to answer your question about what should you do when you grow big.

Can you also tell me what you learned about Buddhism?

Manu: Siddhartha, before becoming famous as Buddha, was a prince. It is believed that there was a prophecy made at the time of his birth that the prince would become a great sage. To prevent this from happening, his father shielded him from suffering and hardship. He was married and had a son.

One day, he saw an old man, a sick man, and a corpse. He was deeply saddened by what he saw. Then, the prince decided to leave his family to search for the truth and meaning of life.

After many years and through deep meditation he attained enlightenment and came to be known as Buddha.

Papa: Do you also remember what his teachings were?

Manu: The four noble truths of Budhha were - Life is full of suffering; this suffering has a cause; the cause of this sorrow is desire, and getting rid of these desires and wants will lead to peace.

Papa: Very good. Seems you know well about these religions. Do you see some relation between what we discussed yesterday and what Mahavira and Buddha did?

Manu: Let me think!!

Yesterday we discussed that we have many desires.

And one of the teachings of Buddha is that desire is the cause of sorrow and getting rid of desire will give us peace. However, I never understood this way though I have read that chapter many times and remembered it also.

Papa: True.

Often, we read our textbooks, remember them well, and also score very good marks. But don't realize how that learning can make our life better.

Religions are about our lives.

Manu: Can you tell me more about religion?

Papa: You told me the name of the Chapter where you learned about Jainism and Buddhism. What was the name of the Chapter in your textbook?

Manu: "Great Thinkers and New Beliefs ".

Papa: Very true.

Both Mahavira and Buddha were great thinkers. They left their houses to learn more about the truths of our life. They wanted to understand the meaning and purpose of our lives, why people suffer, and how to overcome miseries.

So, what exactly were they doing? They were finding answers to these questions. They were searching for knowledge. This is religion.

Religion is the search for knowledge.

Both Mahavira and Buddha were great philosophers.

Manu: Oh! I never thought of religion like this.

Papa: What do we do in science?

Science also seeks knowledge. We want to understand how nature works. Why does a ball when thrown upward come down, how does our body work, how do plants make food, and how do different elements combine to make compounds? These are examples of natural phenomena. Science tries to understand natural phenomena.

While science tries to understand nature, religion tries to understand life.

What is the purpose of life, why do people suffer, what happens to us after death, and what is our origin? Religion tries to find answers to these questions. Today science does not have the tools to answer these questions. There is no conflict between science and religion.

"There is indeed no conflict between being a rigorous scientist and a person who believes in a God who takes a personal interest in each one of us. Science's domain is to explore nature. God's domain is in the spiritual world, a realm inexplorable with the tools and language of science."
– Kalam [1]

Religion finds solutions for people's problems. That too in a scientific way by finding the reason for the problem. That is what Mahavira and Buddha did. They wanted to understand what is the reason for suffering and how to eliminate suffering. We should approach religion with the right perspective.

Manu: But generally, we don't consider religion that way. I thought religion was about going to temples, praying, or some other rituals at home.

Papa: That is what most of us think religion is. That is not the right view. We can understand what is the right meaning of religion.

Actually, religion can answer the question you asked me yesterday- what will you do when you grow up? We will see how.

Manu: Sometimes we discuss if we believe in religion. Some people believe in religion while some people don't. Why is it like that?

Papa: I will try to explain to you with an example. Can you give me an example of something that you want me to get, but you believe I will not get for you?

Manu: Very simple. I have been asking you to get a puppy for me. But you never got it.

Papa: Assume one day, you are at home and Ma and I went out for some work. And after some time, I called you and told you that I got a puppy for you. Will you believe it?

Manu: No. Because I know you will not get it.

Papa: But I insist that I have really got one. Then what will you do?

Manu: I will ask you to show me the Puppy in a video call.

Papa: Suppose I told you that I cannot do a video call now and you will see it when we return home. Then what will you do?

Manu: I will ask you to give the phone to Ma and I will ask Ma if you really bought a puppy.

Papa: Exactly. You won't believe me easily and you want to prove it by seeing yourself or asking Ma if really I got a puppy for you.

Manu: Yes. Because I don't believe you will give me a puppy.

Papa: Similar things happen with religion when it comes to believing in religion.

We hear many things about religion. We also see many religious festivals. We see people praying to statues of different Gods in temples. People say if we do bad things, we will have to come back to earth again. People also talk about a soul within us. God is everywhere and God created us.

But what proof do we have that these things are true? Who has seen them?

If we have seen them or experienced them personally, we will believe in these things. Or if we know someone who has seen or experienced these things and we believe in that person, then also we will believe that these are truths.

It is similar to you seeing the puppy yourself or Ma seeing it and you believe Ma will tell you the truth.

Manu: Has someone seen God?

Papa: If I just say yes, will you believe me? Still, you will have doubts about it.

If our prayers are satisfied, we think God is there. But if our prayers are not satisfied, we think God is not there. That is how many misconceptions about religion develop. So, before I answer this question, let's understand some more things.

Let me ask you another question. How do you recognise a dog as a dog?

Manu: Because I know it is a dog. I have learned how a dog looks. So, I can recognise it when I see a dog.

Perception and Inference are the two common methods of learning. But Intuition is a more powerful method.

Papa: When you were small, Ma or I might have shown a dog to you and told you that this is a dog. After that when you see a dog with your eyes, you can map that image with what you have learned earlier and recognise it. You use your sense of seeing and your intelligence to know that that is a dog. This is how we learn. This way of learning is called Perception.

Suppose you have seen some smoke coming out of a house. What thought comes to your mind?

Manu: Probably there is fire.

Papa: This is because you know that fire produces smoke. This is called Inference. Based on some known facts, learned earlier, we infer new information. Earlier you might have seen fire producing smoke. So now when you see smoke, you infer there is fire.

Perception and Inference are two of the methods that we generally use to gain knowledge.

Both these methods depend on the information received by our senses. We use our senses of seeing, hearing, feeling, tasting or smelling. But our senses have limitations. We can't see everything or hear everything.

The other day while studying physics we were discussing ultrasonic and infrasonic sound. Ultrasonic and Infrasonic waves are not audible to the human ear. With Perception and Inference, we can gain only limited knowledge due to sense limitations.

Manu: But there are instruments that can detect ultrasonic and infrasonic sounds.

Papa: You have a point. Let me try to clarify this.

This is like the chicken and egg problem. For someone to develop an instrument that can detect ultrasonic or infrasonic waves, first should have an idea that there are ultrasonic and infrasonic waves. How do we first know that there are ultrasonic and infrasonic waves?

If you study you can find more information on the Internet. For example, the discovery of ultrasonic waves was inspired by observing and experimenting with how a bat moves at night. Lazzaro Spallanzani, an Italian biologist conducted many experiments in around 1793 and concluded that bats' ability to locate objects while flying does not depend upon their eyes but on their ears. Though he was not sure of the reason, later two other American biologists found that bats produce sound waves whose frequency is higher than what humans can hear. They came up with the concept of echolocation.

Similarly, the discovery of infrasonic sound also has a history where French scientist Vladimir Gavreau and his colleagues observed pain in their eardrums while working in a research lab due to sound waves produced by a lab device, though they were not hearing any sound. Later they discovered that the lab device produces sound waves at a frequency lower than what humans can hear.

Newton discovered gravitational force by observing the apple falling from the tree. The falling apple was seen by his eyes and then using his reasoning and intelligence he proved the existence of gravitational force. This is an example of perception and inference.

The point I am trying to tell you is that first scientists need to get the knowledge. They can obtain knowledge through perception and inference.

The discovery of ultrasonic and infrasonic waves has happened from observations that can be perceived by our senses like the pain in the eardrum or seeing a bat's behaviour. If you study you can find many such examples and later scientists have made many inventions that use such discoveries. These scientific inventions have changed our lives. This is possible because of the developments in science and technology.

But our senses have limits. It is possible that there are things which have not been perceived by our senses or inferred by our intelligence till now. We cannot be sure that we have knowledge of everything.

Once Einstein said, *"What we don't know is much more than what we know"*.

Knowledge of God is one such example. We cannot know God using perception or inference.

In other words, using our intelligence and senses, we cannot know God. That is why even if I explain to you and give reasons that God exists, you will not be able to appreciate it fully. But that does not mean there is no God. At best we don't know.

Manu: How to know God then?

Papa: There is another powerful method of gaining knowledge which does not depend on our senses. It is called Intuition. Intuition is a very powerful tool for acquiring knowledge.

In perception, we gain knowledge from the outside world through sense organs. In inference, we deduce more knowledge by interpreting the information that we receive from the external world through our senses.

For both perception and inference, the source of knowledge is external. In Intuition, we gain knowledge from within. Intuition is direct perception. It does not depend on the senses.

As Intuition does not depend on our senses and knowledge is from within, Intuition is the most powerful method to gain knowledge. Intuition is not reason, it is feeling. We need a clear and calm mind to learn intuitively.

Manu: You said knowledge comes from within. Where is the knowledge then?

Papa: Where is the knowledge? This is a good question.

When Newton discovered gravity after seeing an apple falling in the garden, did he create the gravity force? Gravity already existed. He only discovered that gravity exists.

Physicists are researching subatomic particles and sources of energy inside an atom. They have discovered many more subatomic particles beyond protons, neutrons and electrons, though they are not sure about the exact source of the energy inside the atom. Newly discovered subatomic particles already exist, but someone needs to realize it. The particles are not newly created, only the knowledge is obtained.

Similarly, knowledge about what is the source of atomic energy also exists. Someone needs to realize that. Sometime back we spoke about infrasonic and ultrasonic sound waves.

They existed even before they were discovered, but we did not know that they existed.

"All the knowledge that we have in this world, where did it come from? It was within us. What knowledge is outside? None. Knowledge was not in matter; it was in man all the time. Nobody ever created knowledge; man brings it from within." - Vivekananda [3]

All knowledge already exists. We need the right tool to realize that knowledge.

Imagine a nice shining metal ball obscured by layers of rust. Its shine remains hidden beneath the rust. If you keep removing the rust, slowly the shine will appear. Similarly, knowledge lies within ourselves covered by layers of ignorance. Different life experiences, whether from outside or within, gradually chip away at our ignorance revealing the knowledge within. However, not all ignorance can be dispelled through perception and inference. It is only through intuition that we can eliminate all ignorance and expose the knowledge within.

God cannot be perceived by our senses or understood by our intelligence. God can be known using our intuition.

Manu: You mean we need intuition to know God? Do we have intuition?

Papa: We have, but it is not developed fully. Whatever we call hunches is actually our undeveloped intuition.

For example, you have a feeling you are going to meet your best friend today. This could be your hunch. There is no reason why you think you are going to meet your best friend today, but you have a strong feeling. Often, such hunches or gut feelings turn out to be true.

I will tell you one true story. Ramanujan is a famous Indian mathematician who had great mathematical intuition. In 1913, he sent a letter to British Mathematician G H Hardy of Trinity College, Cambridge which contained 120 formulas and theories. There was no proof of how these formulas were derived.

You have learned about *pi*. We use 3.14 as the value of pi. Actually, the number of digits after the decimal can be many. One of the formulas in that letter was to compute the digits after the decimal value of *pi*. Using his formula and powerful computers, now mathematicians are able to compute 10 trillion decimal positions after the decimal. Another formula from Ramanujan that you can appreciate is finding the number of prime numbers between 1 and any other number.

After receiving the letter, G H Hardy called Ramanujan to the UK and he became a faculty in Trinity College. Unfortunately, Ramanujan died at the very early age of 32 years. Ramanujan wrote those complex mathematical formulas intuitively which still amazes mathematicians and scientists today.

That is the power of intuition.

Manu: You said we have intuition but it is not developed. How can we develop our intuition?

Papa: You already know the answer. I will ask you one more question.

Manu: Papa, you are only asking me questions!

Papa: Yes. I am asking you because I know you already know the answer. But there is a difference between knowing and realising. You may know it but you may not realize it. This discussion will help you to realize this. This is true for many of us.

Manu: I agree. So, what is the question?

Papa: When you explained to me about Jainism and Buddhism, you also told me how Mahavira and Buddha realised the truth. Do you remember that?

Manu: Yes. Buddha was meditating for 49 days continuously at Gaya. Mahavira was also praying for many years.

Papa: Buddha and Mahavira were able to realize the truth by meditating.

Meditation or yoga develops our intuition. You understand consciousness - it is our awareness. Our consciousness can change. For example, our wakeful consciousness is different from when we are sleeping. When we sleep, if we are seeing dreams then we are in a subconscious state and if we are having sound sleep without any dreams, then we are in another state of consciousness. In meditation, our consciousness can change to a higher level.

Our intuitive ability is very subtle and we have very little access to its power in normal wakeful consciousness. In wakeful consciousness, through our senses, we can perceive gross things. But at higher consciousness, we become aware of subtle forces. In meditation, when our consciousness expands to a higher level, our intuition becomes more powerful and we get access to knowledge within us.

Our ancient rishis, who were great thinkers like Buddha and Mahavira, wanted to understand more about life. What is our origin, what is the meaning and purpose of life, and what happens after our death?

Initially, they tried looking outward, trying to understand nature, including the stars. But they could not find answers to these questions. Then they started looking inward.

They sat and concentrated within. As they went deep, making themselves free from all sense distractions, gradually they transcended their consciousness to a higher level and the world of eternal knowledge appeared in front of them. They have heard those inner voices of wisdom.

They acquired this knowledge not by using their sensory perception, but through their intuition at a higher level of consciousness. For many years this knowledge was passed down orally from one individual to another. Later they were written down in the sacred scriptures.

Indian philosophy of *Samkhya* or *Sankhya* is the oldest Philosophy that exists in the world. Kapila, the father of Samkhya philosophy, is considered the first philosopher of the world. As per the Samkhya philosophy, the source of all scriptural knowledge is revealed knowledge. It is revealed to the meditative yogis who attained the highest stage of meditation.

"The second stage of samādhi is called asamprajñāta samādhi. In this state, divine knowledge appears. This is revealed knowledge and it is collected in the scripture called Śruti."
– Kapila [4]

Vedas are the ancient scriptures of the Hindu religion. The word Veda itself means knowledge.

Manu: I have heard about Veda, but I don't know what is written in them. So, what do these scriptures contain?

Papa: They contain the truths about our lives. You have seen examples of Buddha and Mahavira. They went on meditation to understand what is the purpose of life, why people suffer, and how to get rid of life's miseries. You have read in your textbook, that they have found answers to these questions and they were teaching that knowledge to people as religion.

The religious scriptures contain the truths of our life and how we should live our life.

Manu: Still many people don't believe in them?

Papa: Because we need proof to believe in something. Do you believe viruses exist in this world?

Manu: Yes.

Papa: Have you seen the virus yourself?

Manu: No. But I know it can be seen with a microscope. And others have seen it. I have studied this in our biology book.

Papa: So, you know the answer.

The microscope is the tool using which we can see the virus. Though you have not seen it yourself, you know others have seen it. And you have read about it in your biology book.

We need to develop intuition to know the truths of our life. Intuition is the microscope to realize the truths of life. And the Scriptures are the biology book.

If you don't use the microscope or don't read the biology book, can you say there are no viruses? Similarly, just because we don't develop our intuitive ability to realize the truths of our lives and don't read any religious scriptures, can we say that the facts of religion are not true?

Knowledge is important to judge something. Without knowledge, we cannot judge.

If we develop our intuition and study spiritual books, we will not doubt religion anymore.

Manu: I have another question. Why are there so many religions?

Papa: Very good question.

Religion is the search for knowledge. All religions have found truths about our life - who created us, what is the purpose of our life, and where we go after death. Can the answers to these questions be different? If they are different then they are not truths.

Upanishad says, *"Ekam sat, viprahā bahudha vadanti."*. *"Truth is one; seers express it in many ways."*

I have read a book called "The Holy Science" written by Swami Yukteswar Giri. This book shows how Christianity and Hinduism are similar. In that book Swami Yukteswarji said,

"The purpose of this book is to show as clearly as possible that there is an essential unity in all religions; that there is no difference in the truths inculcated by the various faiths; that there is but one method by which the world, both external and internal, has evolved; and that there is but one Goal admitted by all scriptures." [5]

Besides the core truths of the religion, each religion also has mythology and rituals. Mythology and rituals are more concrete, truths are abstract.

Mythology is generally the stories about the legends of the religion while rituals are different ceremonies observed by people. Since mythology and rituals are more concrete in the form of stories and ceremonies, we are more familiar with them than the truth. If I ask you to tell me some mythological stories of the Hindu religion or name a few festivals celebrated by Hindus, you will be able to tell them easily. But, if I ask you what are key teachings of Hinduism are, you will find it difficult to answer.

Mythologies and rituals are different for different religions depending on which part of the world the religion evolved. Diwali is a famous Hindu Festival. Christmas is celebrated by Christians. We are all familiar with these celebrations. But generally, we don't understand the core truths of the religion. So, for common people like us, each religion looks different.

The underlying truths found by all major religions are the same. This underlying truth is spirituality.

"In every religion, there are three parts: philosophy, mythology, and ritual. Philosophy, of course, is the essence of every religion; mythology explains and illustrates it by means of the more or less legendary lives of great men, stories, and fables of wonderful things, and so on; ritual gives to that philosophy a still more concrete form, so that everyone may grasp it — ritual is in fact concretised philosophy. " – Vivekananda [6]

Religion is bound by certain sets of beliefs and recommends different practices. The beliefs and practices of each religion may differ, but spirituality is the common thread across all religions. If we are spiritual seekers, it does not matter which religion we follow. The truth is the same.

In the history of science, there are many examples where the same discovery has been made by two or more scientists independently, but almost simultaneously. This is called "multiple discoveries" or "simultaneous invention". For example, magnetism was discovered independently in Greece, India, and China. But that does not change the properties of magnetism. Magnetism is the same whether it was discovered in Greece, India or China. In the same way, the truths of our lives are the same irrespective of whichever religion realises them. There can be only one truth.

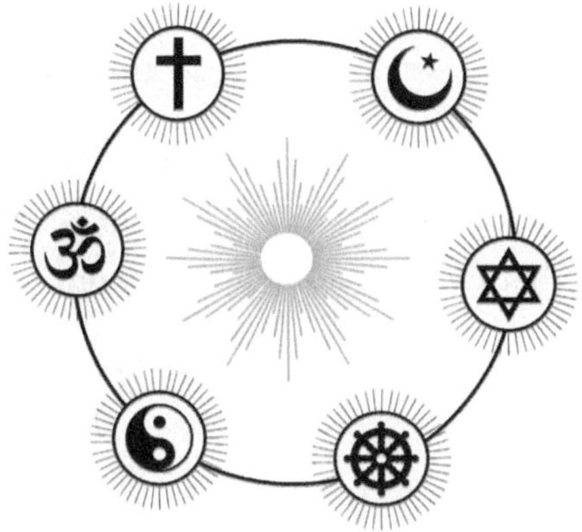

The underlying truth of all religions is Spirituality. Spirituality is the common thread of all religions.

If you remember, earlier we discussed that we don't know our real nature. Because we don't understand our real nature, we don't know what can give us real happiness. And without real happiness, our life is incomplete. We cannot solve our life jigsaw puzzle game.

The religious scriptures contain the truths of our life. By realising these truths, we can know our real nature and find the path to real happiness. In fact, the answer to your question about what you should do when you grow up lies there. We will see how.

Manu: Will you tell me what are those truths of our life?

Papa: Yes. We all should learn these truths found by religion.

They are found scientifically by the ancient yogis and religious prophets and they are the truths of our own life.

They are very close to our hearts. It is not enough to learn them intellectually, we need to realize them intuitively.

Living a life without realising it is like swimming in the sea without having any idea which direction we are going. In fact, that is what most of us are doing in our life.

These truths will show us the direction of our life. We will understand who we actually are, what is the purpose of our life and how to achieve it.

We will have to spend some time learning them. I think it is late for tonight. Let's go and sleep now. We will continue to discuss it tomorrow.

Manu: Oh! Already midnight. Let's sleep. Good night.

Papa: Good night.

• 3 •

Truths of Life

Papa: How was your day today?

Manu: It was good. Actually, I am eagerly waiting to discuss with you something interesting that happened at school today. I don't know whether it is a coincidence or what, but today in our history class Ma'am started a new chapter called Popular Beliefs and Religious Debates. During the class, I remembered what we discussed yesterday evening.

Papa: Oh! That's nice. So, what did you learn in that class today?

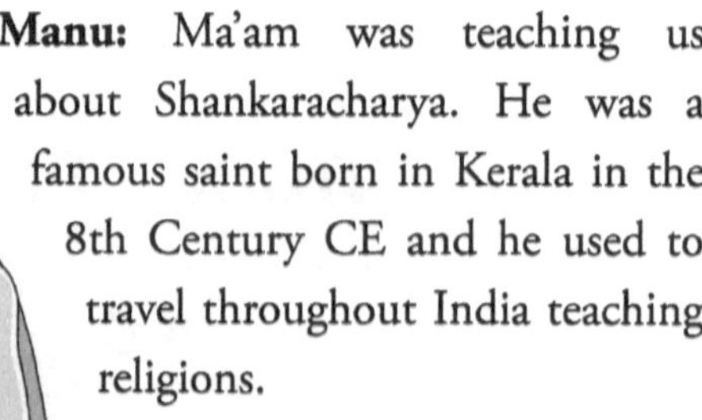

Manu: Ma'am was teaching us about Shankaracharya. He was a famous saint born in Kerala in the 8th Century CE and he used to travel throughout India teaching religions.

Papa: Do you remember what Shankaracharya used to teach?

Manu: I don't remember very clearly. Many concepts were new to me. It is there in the textbook. Shall I get the book?

Papa: Ok. We can look at your textbook.

Manu: Here in the textbook, it is written that Shankaracharya was spreading the importance of jnana or knowledge as a means to reach God. To him, the world was an illusion or Maya. Let me read it directly from the textbook on what he said.

He said, "*One may take delight in yoga or bhoga, may have attachments or detachments. But only he whose mind steadily delights in brahmin enjoys bliss, no one else.*"

Papa: Did you understand the meaning of this?

Manu: Ma'am was explaining more about it and she was discussing God-realisation. She was saying that we can realize God by doing yoga. She also said that the world we see around us is not real.

I understood something, but not very deeply. But I remember you saying yesterday that spiritual knowledge is revealed knowledge. Our ancient rishis have realised them during deep meditation.

Papa: Do you see what we are discussing is something similar to what you are learning in school also?

But maybe we are not going very deep in school and so we are not able to realize how such knowledge can make our life better. Actually, spiritual knowledge can bring a lot of difference to our lives. We will see how.

What you have discussed in class today is an example of what kind of knowledge is there in the scriptures. They talk about God, how to know God, how the creation happened, what happens to us after death etc. These are the truths of our life.

But if we try to understand them only intellectually, we might be able to memorise them and answer the test questions, but we cannot get the real benefits of this divine knowledge. They will not make much difference in our lives.

We need to intuitively realize these truths if we want to make our lives better.

Manu: You said we all should learn this knowledge. This will guide us in our life and I will get an answer to my question about what I should do when I grow big. I want to know exactly what those scriptures contain. What are the truths of our life?

Papa: True. Whatever I am going to explain to you now is revealed knowledge.

Since we are more used to believing in science than religion, some of these facts might sound unbelievable to you. But that is our limitation. We don't have the tools to understand them. You should remember that ancient rishis have gained this knowledge scientifically in a deep meditative state through the power of their intuition. They are true knowledge.

Manu: Yes. I got it. I will listen to you with an open mind.

Papa: That is the right word you said - you will have an open mind. Without an open mind, it will be difficult to appreciate these facts.

If I tell you there is a tiger in the outside park and you believe in me, you will come out to see. It is the belief that is making you take the action of coming out to explore and find out if there is really a tiger in the park. If you don't believe, you will not take any action. So, the first and most important thing is to believe and explore with an open mind.

Manu: Yes. I agree.

Papa: First let's talk about God. Do you believe in God?

Manu: Yes. Definitely, I believe in God.

Papa: In your opinion who is God?

Manu: I think God is a supernatural power. God can do anything. He is everywhere. He is omnipresent and omnipotent.

Papa: Let's try to know more about who God is.

Yesterday we briefly spoke about consciousness. Consciousness is our awareness of internal and external existence. You and I have consciousness. We are aware of our surroundings as well as within us. An unconscious person is not aware of his or her existence or surroundings.

Our consciousness can change. When you are dreaming, you are in a subconscious state. In this state, you can see people or see something happening that is not physically around you. This is different from our normal wakeful conscious state.

Sometimes you also say you had a very good sound sleep. Sound sleep is dreamless deep sleep. In this state, you are not aware of anything happening around you.

Actually, when you are in deep dreamless sleep, your consciousness changes to a different level. That is different from normal consciousness when we are awake or subconsciousness when we see dreams. Because this happens in a deep sleep state, we don't experience it.

Our wakeful consciousness is limited. We are aware of only certain things around us. You don't know what is happening in a far place.

Assume your consciousness can expand and you become aware of everything in the universe. You are aware of you and me sitting together and talking now. But assume you also know what your other friends are doing now though they are not around you. You even know what is happening in another country or another planet. Just imagine. It sounds unrealistic. But actually, it is possible.

It is possible to expand our awareness. We can become aware of the universe the way we are now aware of this room. We will learn how it happens.

What is there beyond the Universe? Infinity. Assume your consciousness can become infinite. Then you will know what is there beyond the Universe. This Infinite Consciousness is God or Spirit. This is also called Cosmic Consciousness.

Cosmic Consciousness pervades everything in the Universe and beyond it. That is why we say God is everywhere. He is Omnipresent.

God is Infinite Consciousness.

Manu: So, God is not a person?

Papa: God can manifest as a person like us. For example, Jesus Christ and Bhagwan Krishna are manifestations of God.

In fact, everything in the Universe, including humans, nature, plants and animals, and the stars and planets are manifestations of God. Everything has originated from this Infinite Consciousness. We will learn more about it as we continue our discussion.

Manu: Who created God? And when?

Papa: I was expecting this question from you. That is the most obvious question that comes to our mind.

If you see a new flower bouquet on the table you will ask who got it. The flower bouquet cannot come on its own, someone has to bring it.

Why is the bulb glowing? Because electricity is passing through the bulb. The bulb cannot glow without a reason.

There has to be a reason for everything. Nothing happens without reason. We are used to this pattern of thinking. This is what we have learned. There is nothing wrong with this. But is this always true?

Attributing a cause or reason to everything is called cause and effect phenomena.

Why does the apple fall? Due to gravity. Gravity is the cause and the apple falling down is the effect. Because Newton thought there had to be a reason why the apple came down and did not go up, he discovered gravity.

Imagine something can happen without a reason also. Then our thinking pattern will change. We will not ask who or why.

In Absolute, there is no cause and effect. There is no change in Absolute. Infinite Consciousness of God or Cosmic Consciousness is Absolute. There is no change in Cosmic Consciousness.

The change started from Cosmic Consciousness when the universe was created. So, the idea of cause and effect applies in the Universe, not beyond the Universe. Cosmic Consciousness is changeless and beyond cause and effect. There cannot be any reason why God exists. So, who created God will not have any answer.

Without change, time has no meaning. Time measures change. There was no change before the creation of the Universe. It was changeless. There was no concept of time before the Universe was created. The question of when will not have any answer where there is no concept of time itself. That is why since when God exists cannot have any answer.

"For in the Absolute, there is neither time, space, nor causation; It is all one. That which exists by itself alone cannot have any cause. That which is free cannot have any cause; else it would not be free, but bound." – Vivekananda [7]

Manu: How does God look? Can we see him?

Papa: For something to have a look must have a shape. Infinite does not have any shape. It is omnipresent. God is infinite. He has no form and shape.

But God can take any shape. God manifests in different forms.

As I mentioned before, the entire Universe is His manifestation. We are also His manifestations. We need to learn more to understand what exactly this means. Let's continue our discussion and you will learn it as we progress.

God is Absolute. Time, space, and causation do not apply to God.

This may sound very crazy to you because you are so familiar with time, space, and cause and effect. It is hard for you to imagine something where time, space, and causation do not apply. That is our limitation to perceive.

Earlier we discussed perception, inference, and intuition. Some facts are difficult to perceive with an intelligent mind due to our sense limitations. That is why it is difficult for science to comprehend God. But with Intuition, it is possible.

We need to develop our intuition to appreciate these facts fully. Ancient rishis could realize them using their developed intuitive power through meditation.

Ancient philosopher of India Kapila said that by meditating we can realize the cause of this universe. This is how ancient Rishis could know the cause of the universe.

"The subtle causes can be seen with inner vision. This inner vision is pure wisdom and it is attained through meditation. In meditation, we establish ourselves in the Knower who knows both the manifest and unmanifest. The Knower is able to observe because it is beyond Nature. Settled within, a person is able to realize three things: the root cause of this universe, the effects of this root cause, and his or her own real self as the Knower of both." – Kapila [4]

Manu: How did the creation start from God?

Papa: Suppose you want to create something. For example, a toy car. What will you do?

First, you will have an idea in your mind that you want to create something. But only with the ideas, you will not be able to create the car. You need some materials also.

In science, you have learned that matter consists of atoms and molecules. The atoms consist of further smaller subatomic particles. You have studied electrons, protons, and neutrons. According to the research in particle physics, the fundamental subatomic particles are energy quantum.

Quark is believed to be the most fundamental particle as per the latest research. Quark cannot be seen independently, it can be seen only in groups. Quark is energy quantum.

The fundamental energy quantum appears as gross particles and forms atoms and molecules. The atoms and molecules form the matter that is part of the visible Universe. It is already proven in science that all matter comes from energy.

From this, you can understand that creation involves three parts - idea, energy, and matter. We are familiar only with the matter part. From where does the idea come and what is the source of the energy? Let's try to understand that.

First God had an idea that He wanted to create something. This idea was in the Cosmic Consciousness of God, similar to how our thoughts are in our consciousness. Before this, there was no change. This was the first change in the otherwise changeless state of Cosmic Consciousness. This was the beginning of Creation.

Our thoughts are a subtle force. This thought of creation in God's Consciousness is also a force. Forces are vibrations. So, this first creative force in God's Consciousness is also a vibration. With this vibration, the concept of change, space, time, and causation started. Vibration is a change. Change means time. Vibration has happened in some spaces. And there was a reason for this change. The reason was God's Will to create something.

Paramahansa Yoganandaji has termed this subtle creative energy, emanating from God's Consciousness, as "thoughtrons". Thoughts are very subtle. These subtle thoughtrons became grosser and manifested as "lifetrons". Lifetrons are the fundamental force or energy from where everything else in the universe is created. So, the source of all energy and consequently the matter that we see in the universe originates from Cosmic Consciousness [2].

Cosmic Consciousness is the source of all creation. Subtle energy emanating from Cosmic Consciousness condenses and finally appears as the gross matter that we see around us.

Max Planck, a German theoretical physicist, who got the Nobel Prize for his contribution to Quantum Physics once said, *"As a man who has devoted his whole life to the most clear-headed science, to the study of matter, I can tell you as a result of my research about atoms this much: There is no matter as such. All matter originates and exists only by virtue of a force, which brings the particle of an atom to vibration and holds this most minute solar system of the atom together. We must assume behind this force the existence of a conscious and intelligent mind. This mind is the matrix of all matter."* [8]

All matter exists due to force or energy. Behind this force, there is a Conscious and Intelligent mind. That is God.

Scientists have been working for many years to understand how consciousness originates in our brains. But there is no convincing explanation for that till now. This is called the *hard problem of consciousness*. After the discovery of quantum physics, some scientists and psychologists have started doubting if matter is really fundamental to everything we see in the universe.

Max Planck also said, "*I regard consciousness as fundamental. I regard matter as derivative from consciousness. We cannot get behind consciousness. Everything that we talk about, everything that we regard as existing, postulates consciousness.*" *[9]*

There is a famous experiment in quantum physics called the double-slit experiment. In this experiment, scientists have observed that the behaviour of a particle changes when it is observed. Though there is no single explanation for this behaviour, many scientists believe that the behaviour of the particle is influenced by the consciousness of the observer.

As science develops, I believe that one-day science also will have the same conclusion that consciousness is the source of all energy. There is no conflict between science and spirituality. They complement each other.

As we discussed sometime before, the three parts of creation or existence are idea, energy, and gross matter. They are called causal, astral, and physical respectively. They are the same, emanating from the Cosmic Consciousness of God, only differing in frequency.

It is similar to how we call different frequency spectrums of electromagnetic waves visible light, X-rays, and ultraviolet rays. The energy from Cosmic Consciousness appears in different forms because of different frequencies. Causal is very subtle, astral is grosser than causal, and physical is the grossest manifestation.

In our wakeful consciousness, we are aware of the physical world. We cannot perceive the astral and causal world in normal consciousness. But at a higher level of consciousness, the astral and causal world becomes visible to us.

We can learn this from Bhagavad Gita. *"The physical world is in reality nothing more than inert matter. The inherent life and animation in all forms, from atoms to man, come from the subtle forces of the astral world. These, in turn, have evolved from the still finer forces of the causal or ideational creation, the creative vibratory thoughts emanating from the consciousness of God." [2]*

All creations have causal, astral, and physical aspects.

Nature, which is the first creation from the Cosmic Consciousness of God, has a causal nature, an astral nature, and a physical nature. The causal nature or *para-prakriti,* as it is called in the scriptures, has the intelligence and consciousness of God that governs the entire creation. Astral nature has the subtle cosmic energy or life energy that powers and sustains the entire universe. The physical nature is what we see around us.

Similarly, you and I also have the causal body, the astral body, and the physical body. The causal body provides us with intelligence and consciousness, the astral body provides us with the life energy or prana for our physical body to function and the physical body is what we are familiar with. We will discuss this in more detail a little later.

Manu: How about Big Bang Theory? Is the Universe not created because of the Big Bang?

Papa: Lots of work is happening in science to understand the origin of the universe. Big Bang is probably the most popular and accepted theory.

The Universe has unfolded after the Big Bang. The theories of science can explain this unfolding. But that is not creation. What was there before the Big Bang?

There is no theory now that can predict completely what the Universe was before the Big Bang though there are many ideas. There are different theories proposed and discussed over the years, but there are many unanswered questions as well.

There is no conflict here. Today science has tools to understand and explain nature. Unfolding of the universe after the Big Bang or any other event for that matter is part of nature that can be intellectually explained by science.

But what is beyond the Universe is beyond nature. Today science does not have the tools to perceive that. It is beyond the capability of our senses.

Tools in spirituality are not limited by our senses. So, Spirituality can realize what is there beyond nature. Maybe in the future science will also have tools to understand what is beyond nature.

Manu: Sometime back you said nature has intelligence. How can nature have intelligence?

Papa: Every day you follow a routine. You wake up in the morning, get ready to go to school, finish your breakfast on time, and board your school bus. In school, you know which classroom you should enter; when you take breaks, and when you should return back home. Afternoon you go out to play with your friends. If you observe, your work happens in an orderly manner every day. Who drives this order? It is your intelligence.

Like you do your things in an orderly way, everything in nature also happens in an orderly manner.

From the stars in the sky to the subatomic particles inside an atom follows a certain order. The roots of the tree are under the soil to absorb water and the leaves are above the ground so that they can receive sunlight to prepare food. If you look around nature, you will find many such things that happen in an orderly manner. There is food for all species. Death happens naturally. If there were no death, what would have happened to Earth? Have you ever thought about how it happens like this?

As you do everything in an orderly way because of your Intelligence, everything in nature also happens in an orderly manner because of Cosmic Intelligence. Everything in the universe is governed by Cosmic Intelligence.

Like us, the universe is also an organism with its own intelligence. Like our body has a mechanism to sustain it of its own, the universe also has its own mechanism of sustaining it.

There is a theory among philosophers called panpsychism supporting this view of the universe. Whether the universe is a machine or an organism is a debatable topic among scientists without any conclusion now. But spiritual knowledge says that the Universe is a living thing with its own Intelligence and Consciousness.

The universe is the macrocosm and our body is the microcosm.

Manu: Can you tell me more about our body? We have learned about our respiratory system and digestive system. While studying about our bodies I was wondering how our bodies can work so smartly.

Papa: Our body is a very sophisticated system.

In our view, our body works involuntarily. We eat food and our digestive system works to digest the food and give us energy. We don't ask the digestive system, saying, "Hey! Now digest the food and give me energy". When we are in deep sleep, we breathe. Otherwise, we would not have gotten up from sleep at all. How do these things happen involuntarily?

Inside the mother's womb, for most babies, the body grows nicely with all body parts in the proper place, of the proper dimensions. Where does this intelligence come from? We also think, recognise different objects, judge good and bad, feel happy or sad, and get angry. How does it happen? How is the body designed so intelligently and who has designed it?

Let me try to explain to you with an example.

Nowadays you can do so many things using a smartphone. You open an app and type something and your friend in another place can reply immediately. You can play online games with your friends. You can order groceries, and buy clothes using the phone. If you don't understand how the phone works, to you it will look like everything is happening automatically. But actually, there is programmed hardware and software that makes the phone function the way it is functioning.

The phone will switch off if there is no charge. The charge provides the electrical energy for the phone to function. Our body also works because of prana or life energy. Without prana, the body will die. Prana or life force is a subtle current. Because of prana, our digestive system works when we eat food, we continue to breathe when we are in deep sleep, and our senses work.

We have another subtle body called the energy body or astral body behind our physical body.

The energy body consists of "*nadis*" and "*chakras*". Like the electricity flows in the electrical circuits of the phone, this life current flows in the "*nadis*" and "*chakras*" of our energy body and makes our physical body work the way it is working now.

The astral or energy body has a similar shape to our physical body. Like our physical brain, there is an astral brain in our cerebrum called "*sahasrara*". And similar to our physical spine, there is an astral spine called "*sushuma*". Besides "*sahasrara*" there are six other subtle energy centres called "*chakras*" along the astral spine. The life force works through these "*chakras*".

The energy body gives us the power to do bodily functions similar to the electricity in the phone. But we also need intelligence. In the phone, intelligence is programmed by people. Where does our body get intelligence from?

This intelligence comes from Cosmic Consciousness.

As we discussed, creation starts with an idea in the consciousness of God. This idea also has a subtle structure and is called our causal body. It is the cause of the energy body and the gross physical body.

Cosmic Consciousness manifests as the "*soul*" in the causal body. The soul gives us divine intelligence and consciousness.

Manu: I thought the soul is inside our body. How does it enter our body?

Papa: Soul is the individualised consciousness of God.

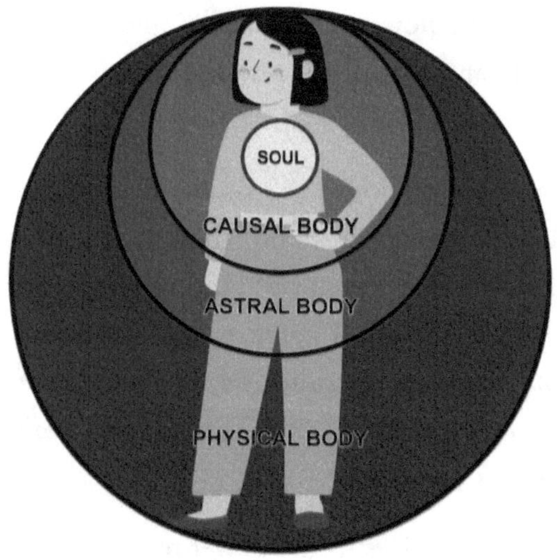

Within our Physical body, we have Astral and Causal bodies. Our Soul is encapsulated within the Causal body.

The soul inside the causal body first forms an astral body around it. Only with the astral body, the soul can manifest in gross forms. Along with the causal and astral body, the soul enters our physical body inside our mother's womb. So, the physical body gets the intelligence and consciousness to grow as a human body.

The causal body also follows a similar shape to our physical body. We have a causal brain which is the centre of our wisdom. We spoke about intuition earlier. The causal medulla is the centre of intuition. There are five other *chakras* in the causal spine where our consciousness manifests as other subtle forces such as calmness and power of self-control and self-restraint.

"What we call our body actually has three layers of body. The physical body, the energy body or astral body and the causal body". We can learn this from Bhagavad Gita [2].

The physical body is the gross matter, the astral body is life energy or prana and the causal body is idea or thought – the three aspects of creation as we discussed sometime back. The source of all of them is Cosmic Consciousness. We don't realize the astral body and causal body in our normal consciousness.

The physical body is part of nature. It can be explained in the language of biology and chemistry. But the subtle bodies behind the physical body cannot be comprehended by intelligence today. So they are called the spiritual body. Our physical body will not work without the spiritual body.

Science can treat the physical body, but when life force or prana leaves our body, science cannot bring them back.

Manu: How about other species like plants and animals? Are they also like us?

Papa: I will tell you. Have you sometimes received a birthday gift that was wrapped in multiple covers? Do you remember the experience of opening the gift?

Manu: Yes. We need to open multiple layers of gift wraps before we actually see the gift. It is exciting to guess what the gift is while removing the wrapped papers one by one. I have done that many times and even my friends used to wait eagerly to see what was inside.

Papa: True. First, you remove the outermost colourful gift wrap paper. Then probably you see a cardboard box. Once you open the cardboard box, you find the bubble wrap cover. Then you open the bubble wrap cover to find the actual gift.

Unless you open the colourful gift paper, you don't see what is inside. As you remove the outside cover, the next cover reveals to you.

As we pack the gift inside many layers of gift wrapping, our soul is also covered by multiple layers of covers. These covers are called the sheaths or "*koshas*". There are five layers of sheaths covering our soul.

The outermost layer is our gross body or "*Annamaya kosha*" that we are aware of. Inside this is called the "*Pranamaya kosha*" or life sheath in our astral body. We are generally not fully aware of our prana though prana is continuously working in our astral body.

Awareness and conscious control of the life force is necessary to realize our inner world.

Next is the "*Manomaya kosha*" or mind sheath. Because of our minds, we perceive things. Our mind connects us to the external world through our senses. If we train our minds, the same mind can connect us to the internal world using our intuitive ability.

Behind that is the "*Jnanamaya kosha*" or Intellect sheath. When we get access to this layer, we get divine wisdom. Our intellect becomes discriminative and we can judge good and bad. Without that, we are intelligent but not wise.

The innermost layer is the bliss sheath or "*Anandamaya kosha*". When we are able to use our discriminative intelligence and control our minds, we get access to this layer. This is when we know our soul which was covered inside all these layers.

There are five koshas covering our soul. The outermost kosha is called Annamaya kosha, then Pranamaya kosha, Manomaya kosha, Jnanamaya and the innermost is Anandamaya kosha.

Knowing the soul is the soul consciousness. This is our true nature, our real self.

In normal situations, we live in the wakeful consciousness when we are aware of the outside world. If we want to know our true nature, we need to open these sheaths that cover our souls. Otherwise, we will never realize who we are, as you will not know what the gift is unless you remove all the gift wrapping.

You said it is exciting to guess what the gift is while opening the gift wraps, but it is a thousand times more exciting to know your soul. No other experience in the world can compensate for that. Realising the soul consciousness is bliss.

Only for humans is it possible to realise the soul. In inert matter, for example, a stone, none of the layers are revealed. So it is just an inert matter. In a plant, there is life but no mind and consciousness. Animals have minds and consciousness, but no intelligence to judge good and bad. Humans have intelligence.

Poet and Mystic Philosopher Ibn Arabi said, *"God sleeps in the rock, dreams in the plant, stirs in the animal, and awakens in man"*.

When our intelligence becomes discriminative as we develop our intuition and get access to divine wisdom, we can realize our soul nature.

Manu: This seems a bit complex to me now to understand!!

Papa: Don't worry. They are complex. And when we try to understand them with our intellect, they appear even more complex. That is the limitation of our intelligence.

"The field of reason, or of the conscious workings of the mind, is narrow and limited. There is a little circle within which human reason must move. It cannot go beyond. Every attempt to go beyond is impossible, yet it is beyond this circle of reason that there lies all that humanity holds most dear. All these questions, whether there is an immortal soul, whether there is a God, whether there is any supreme intelligence guiding this universe or not, are beyond the field of reason. Reason can never answer these questions." [10]

We need to go beyond the limited circle of reason to understand life. Only with the intuitive ability we can go beyond this circle. Ancient rishis have realised this knowledge through intuition, not through reason or intelligence.

It is expected that you will find it complex to understand. Even though it is a bit difficult for you to understand now, I still prefer to give you some ideas about it. There is a reason for it.

Manu: What is the reason?

Papa: Though you understand part of it now, this will strengthen your belief in spirituality. You will appreciate the profoundness of spiritual knowledge.

We have a curious and doubting mind. If I just tell you our body works so smartly because of God, you will not appreciate it so much. But when you have an idea of the details of how the consciousness and intelligence of God are making our body perform different functions through the causal and energy body, then you will appreciate it better.

A similar thing happens when you study science. You try to understand the concepts to understand why a natural phenomenon happens the way it happens. As science is a more accepted realm, we tend to believe scientific facts more easily.

Spiritual facts are harder to believe, unlike scientific facts. Also, many superficial religious practices with a vested interest that we see around us have done more harm to authentic knowledge of spirituality. People with rational minds tend not to believe spiritual facts.

But as we discussed in the last few days, spirituality is beyond our intellectual reasoning. We need intuitive understanding to appreciate spiritual knowledge. Since our intuition is not developed so much, it becomes like a vicious cycle. Spiritual practices will develop our intuition. But if we wait to appreciate all spiritual knowledge, before we start spiritual practices then we will always be in that vicious cycle. We need to start somewhere.

I am sure by now you are able to see the science behind spiritual facts. Though you don't understand it fully now, you are probably beginning to appreciate that the spiritual facts are scientific. This is the point I am trying to make by telling you more details.

Believing in spirituality is very important. This will make us learn more and practice more. It is like believing that there is a tiger in the park and coming out to see it. I am telling you that there is a tiger in the park. You need to come out and see if there is really a tiger in the park.

As we learn more and practice more, it will not be just belief, but the realisation of the knowledge. This is a good starting point. We need to start it early in our life. Otherwise, we can never enjoy the benefits of spirituality and make our lives better.

Manu: I agree. I have another question. Sometime back you spoke about the soul. I have heard the word soul earlier also. Recently I saw an animated movie called "Soul". Can you tell me more about the soul?

Papa: Yes. Soul is a commonly used word.

To refer to a good person, sometimes people say great soul. Similarly, you might have heard people praying for the soul to rest in peace after the death of someone.

So, what did you see in the movie "Soul"?

Manu: In that movie, they showed that after death the soul goes to another place where either it will die or it can again come back to earth. If the soul goes to a place called "great beyond" it will die. In another place called "great before," they prepare the souls to come back to earth and give them an earth pass.

Papa: Interesting. Something similar to that happens to our souls also. Let's try to understand what the soul is.

You can see the reflection of the moon in a glass of water. If you keep multiple glasses, you will see multiple images of the moon. If one glass breaks and water spills away, the image will disappear. But the moon is still there. If you bring another glass of water, you will again see the image of the moon.

Our soul is like that. It enters our body at the time of creation inside the mother's womb. At the time of death, the soul leaves the body and later might enter another physical body. The soul is an image of Cosmic Consciousness or God.

There can be many souls as there can be many images of the moon. But they are all images of one Cosmic Consciousness or God. Even if our physical body dies, like the glass is broken, the soul can again appear in another body, similar to the image of the moon appearing in another glass of water.

Manu: What happens to the soul after our death?

Papa: I will tell you. Have you heard of stories about near-death experiences?

Manu: I remember you telling the story about one American neurosurgeon who was in a coma for seven days and later recovered. During those seven days, he experienced things that we don't experience in this world. You also told me that there he met his sister, whom he never met on earth.

Papa: Yes. That is one such example that I read about in the book "Proof of Heaven" by Dr Eben Alexander. But there are many such experiences where people feel like leaving their body and experiencing something very different, kind of calm and good feeling. This happens when they meet with some life-threatening incident like a heart attack or some kind of trauma.

Some people experiencing such near-death experiences have said that they felt like going through a tunnel and experiencing something like a very bright light at the end of the tunnel. And they feel they are beyond time and space. They could even meet people from their family who died a long time back.

There is a lot of research happening about it and you will find a lot of information related to this. This is another example that science finds difficult to explain. However, as we will learn, spirituality can explain such experiences.

Your soul, which is part of eternal consciousness, can leave the physical body but still retain the consciousness. The soul continues to live inside the causal and astral body. Something similar to this happens during near-death experiences.

To understand what happens to the soul after death, we need to understand another truth of our life. Karmic law or the Law of Karma determines what happens to the soul after death.

The Law of Karma is a Cosmic Law.

Manu: I have heard the word Karma. What is the Law of Karma?

Papa: A scientific law defines a physical phenomenon that always happens in a certain way. For example, if you apply force on an object, the object moves or tends to move in the direction of the force. This is a scientific law. Based on different observations and experiments, Newton observed that this is always true. So, this became a universal law. You have studied this in physics.

A law in science explains physical phenomena and predicts the result. Unlike scientific law, cosmic law explains a cosmic phenomenon and predicts the result. The Law of Karma is a Cosmic Law. Science deals with only nature while spirituality deals with entire life. The law of karma is about our life.

Newton's third law of force states that for every action there is an equal and opposite reaction. The Karmic law is similar to that.

As you sow, so shall you reap. Our actions are called *karma*. But here, we will call the results of our actions as karma. The good work that we do gives us good karma and the bad work that we do gives us bad karma. It is not just the action, but also our thoughts. Even bad thoughts add to bad karma and good thoughts add to good karma.

Our karma is the sum total of the results of all our work.

Karma is not only related to our current life. Based on our past lives we already have some accumulated karma, called *Sanchita Karma.*

Our past karma decides our current life. Where we are born, our nature, health, etc are decided by our past karma.

We live in an eternal life cycle that consists of a physical, astral, and causal world. Our own work influences this life cycle.

In our current life, based on our work we earn more karma called *Agami Karma.* Our past karma and our work in this life decide our fate after death. They are stored as impressions in our consciousness called *samskaras.*

Our soul is encased within the causal, astral, and physical body. Corresponding to these three bodies, there are three worlds. We are living in the physical world. After death, we will go to the astral world.

These worlds are not separated by physical distance like how India and the US are separated. They are separated by the frequency of energy. The physical world is the most gross, the astral world is subtle while the causal world is even subtler. We have learned about it while discussing the stages of creation.

When we die, our physical body will die. But the astral body continues to live in the astral world. And the soul will be inside the astral and causal body.

After many years, depending on our karma, the astral body will come back to earth again entering another physical body. It has to find a matching body as per the karmic results. This continues till the time we free all our karma. Then the astral body need not come back to earth.

However, we still have the causal body. The soul is inside the causal body. When we have very little karma left, we will go back to the causal world. This happens when the astral body dies. The soul may come back to the astral world again.

Eventually, at the death of the causal body, the soul unites with God. A causal body is nothing but ideas. Death of the causal body means the ideas won't be there but the consciousness still remains. Thus, the individualised consciousness of God becomes the same as the Cosmic Consciousness.

The earth is a learning school for us. The law of karma helps us to learn. Once we complete our learning we don't need to come back again to this school. If we don't want rebirth, we need to follow the law of karma and make ourselves free from karma.

The astral world is something similar to what you have seen in the movie "Soul". The souls live there inside the astral body. Also, as you have seen in the movie, the soul prepares to come back to earth and will wait for its turn. As per their karma, when they find a match, they will get the Earth pass to come back to Earth.

I will tell you a story - a real story.

Manu: Please. I like to listen to stories.

Papa: Paramahansa Yogananda was a famous spiritual leader of India. Swami Yukteswar was his guru. In 1920, Paramahansa Yogandanji went to the US to teach Self-Realisation in the West. He came back to India in 1935 for a trip. During his stay in India, his guru, Swami Yuketeswar died on 9th March 1936. The story I am going to tell you now is from the book "Autobiography of a Yogi" by Paramahansa Yogananda. [11]

After death, Swami Yukeswar was cremated in Puri. Yoganandji was also there during the cremation. Later, in June 1936, Paramahansa Yoganandaji was supposed to return back to the US from Mumbai. However due to some reason, his plan got canceled, and he was staying in the Regent Hotel in Mumbai.

As he was meditating in his hotel room, on 19 June 1936, suddenly he was awakened from meditation by a blissful light. When he opened his eyes, he saw his guru Swami Yukteswar, in the same flesh and blood as he was before his death. This happened almost three months after his death. Paramahansa Yogananda hugged his guru and they spoke for two hours in that hotel room. During that discussion, Swami Yukteswar explained how the astral world is to Paramahansa Yogananda.

Not all souls in the astral world can appear in the same physical body after death. But Swami Yukteswar was a more evolved soul so he could take his physical body form at will and could talk to his disciple Paramahansa Yogananda.

Manu: Wow!! I can't believe this!!

Papa: Yes. Difficult to believe but true.

As we discussed earlier, everything in the Universe is energy. Matter is also energy. God created everything in this universe from the energy emanating from his Consciousness using his willpower. Advanced yogis, those who can transcend their consciousness to God Consciousness and remain in that consciousness have such spiritual power. That is how Swami Yukteswar could materialise the energy and take the form of his physical body. You can see the science behind such stories. They are true and real.

Manu: Yes. Often, we think such stories are not true. But now I am starting to believe that they are more scientific. I am still thinking about my first question. What should I do when I grow up? You said knowledge of spirituality will help me to get an answer to my question. I am still not sure how.

Papa: You keep reminding me of your question. We should find the answer from our discussion at the right time. Spirituality is about our life. Spiritual knowledge should give direction to our lives and make our lives better. Otherwise, how does it help us? So, we should definitely find an answer to your question.

As we discussed earlier, you need to know your true nature before you decide what you should do when you grow up.

If we don't understand our true nature, we don't know what can give us real happiness in life.

Sometime back we talked about our souls. Our soul is our true nature. Generally, we are not aware of soul consciousness. In wakeful hours, we are more conscious of our body and senses. As the senses connect us to the external world, we are conscious of the external world.

We need to realize our true nature, which is soul consciousness.

Manu: How to realize our true nature?

Papa: We will talk about that. But before that, we need to know why in the first place we don't know our true nature. If soul consciousness is our true nature, then why is our wakeful consciousness different from soul consciousness?

Manu: Oh, I did not think about that!!

Papa: No Problem. I will explain it to you.

We spoke about the astral and causal bodies sometime back. They are subtle bodies working along with our physical body. The soul along with the causal and astral body enters our physical body inside our mother's womb.

You remember we discussed that the astral body has the astral brain and six other chakra. Initially, the life force from the astral brain flows downward enabling all the astral chakras along the astral spine and reaching the bottommost chakra called coccygeal or *muladhara*. This life force resting in the *muladhara chakra* is called *Kundalini.* We all have the Kundalini force resting in our *muladhara.* From *muladhara,* life energy moves to other body parts and senses and thus our senses get activated.

Along with life force, soul consciousness also moves downward from the causal brain through the causal spine and moves to other body parts and senses. Thus, we become aware of our body and senses.

This is how soul consciousness becomes body consciousness. The senses connect us to the external world. We become aware of the external world.

As we become aware of our body and senses and get connected with the external world, we forget our internal nature. We get busy with the external world and forget soul consciousness, which is our true nature. As souls, we are made in the image of God. But when we recognise ourselves as body, we think we are different from God. Because we think we are separate from God and become independent, we are called ego which means "I". Body consciousness is also called ego consciousness. [2]

This is called delusion or Maya. We don't recognise our true nature, which is the soul and we think we are ego.

If you see a rope in the darkness, you might think of it as a snake. The rope appears as a snake in the darkness. Similarly, due to our ignorance, the soul appears as ego.

Delusion is the root cause of most of the problems we face in this world.

Due to this delusion, we don't know who we are and what exactly we want in our lives. Senses connect us to the external material world. Thinking of ourselves as ego and identifying with the body and senses, we seek all material things in this world. We think achieving these material things is the purpose of our life and we can get happiness from them. This is where we go wrong in our life jigsaw puzzle game.

Ego is our apparent nature, but soul is our true nature.

First of all, we cannot get real happiness from them. Material things can satisfy our ego but not our soul. So, they will not fit that mandatory piece of the puzzle that we are looking for. That slot will still remain empty. That is why we still feel that emptiness within us even after having many material achievements.

Secondly, as we try to get more and more of these material things, we make the game more complex. We violate the hidden rule of the game. It will become more difficult for us to find that mandatory piece of happiness now. This is what is happening to us in our lives.

We are like those people before the invention of the wheel, dragging a heavy load on a surface to move from one place to another, without knowing that wheels can make it easier. They were ignorant. We are trying to achieve many material things and love and care from others thinking that can give us real happiness, without knowing that they cannot satisfy our soul. They can satisfy only our ego. We are ignorant.

Another good analogy of this is the sea and its waves. The waves are made from seawater. But we don't call them the sea, we call them waves. Actually, they are different forms. When the wave is gone it becomes sea. The waves cannot be there without the sea. But the sea can be there without the waves.

We are like the waves, appearing in different forms from the sea of Cosmic Consciousness. Everything in the Universe is different manifestations of Cosmic Consciousness taking different forms as inert objects, plants, animals, people, and even the stars and planets. Like the waves lose their forms and become sea, everything in the universe also becomes Cosmic Consciousness after losing the manifested form. Cosmic Consciousness is always there like the sea. Its manifestations may or may not be there, similar to the waves.

The waves, when identified as waves, do not have the power of the sea. Similarly, when we are identified as different objects in the universe, we lose the power of God.

Abdul Kalam said, *"It begins with the awareness of the true nature of human experience: you are a soul, but you experience life through the senses of the body." [1]*

Manu: God is very powerful and he knows everything. Then why did God not solve this problem of delusion? Why did He create this problem in the first place?

Papa: This is not only your question. Most of us trying to understand spirituality and the truths of life have this question. Why did God leave us with this problem?

This is discussed in many spiritual books. God realised yogis and rishis understand the reason. I will try to answer from what I have learned.

Unless we free ourselves from delusion, we cannot understand completely why God created this delusion in the first place. When we are in delusion, we cannot see the world the way God sees it. We need to learn to see the world the way He is seeing it. Then we can understand why God created delusion in the first place.

In the calm ocean, a storm is needed to form the waves. Storm creates differentiated waves from the undifferentiated ocean. Similarly, the cosmic maya or delusion is needed to create differentiated beings from the undifferentiated Cosmic Consciousness.

Delusion is required for the creation.

Have you observed that everything in the universe has an opposite? This is called dual nature or duality. There is good and bad, day and night, birth and death, light and dark, knowledge and ignorance, healthy and sick, happy and unhappy, restless and calm, and so on. So are their soul and ego. Delusion is the cause of this duality. As souls, we are made of the image of God. This delusion makes us different from God. Without delusion, we will violate the rule of nature. Delusion is needed to follow the rule of nature.

But we are not helpless. We are only ignorant. If we have the wisdom, we know how to free ourselves from this delusion. This wisdom is there in spiritual knowledge, though it is not there today in science or philosophy.

This world is a learning school for us. God wants us to learn and go back to him. He does not want us to stay here for a long time. To enable us to return back to him, he has given us free will. We have free will. He does not force anything on us. If we use our free will correctly, we can free ourselves from this delusion and return to him. If we misuse our free will and live in delusion for a long time, we cannot blame God for that. [15]

Manu: What exactly do we need to do in order to free ourselves from delusion?

Papa: By throwing light on the rope, we can know that it is not a snake but a rope only. Light helps us to remove our delusions. Similarly, with the light of knowledge, we can free ourselves from delusion and realise our true nature. This knowledge comes from spirituality and the practice of spirituality.

Knowledge and practice of spirituality will help you to understand your true nature. We are on the right track to answering your original question.

It will take some more time for me to explain to you what exactly we need to do to free ourselves from delusion. It is very late today. Let's go and sleep. Tomorrow we will discuss more. Good night.

Manu: Good night.

• 4 •

Path to Happiness

Papa: Let's start our discussion today with a very simple question. If someone asks you to introduce yourself, how will you introduce yourself?

Manu: That is not difficult. I will say I am Manasvi Nath. I am a student studying in class nine at National Public School. I live in Bengaluru.

Papa: Similarly, I will introduce myself as Ranjit Nath. I am an engineer working for a so-and-so company. I live in Bengaluru.

Our identities are our name, what we do, and where we live. If someone has received a big award, say the Nobel Prize, she will be introduced as a Nobel laureate. A rich person with billions of money will be introduced as a billionaire.

What we have acquired after we came to this world has become our identity.

Do you remember who you are when you are sleeping? But the moment you wake up, you will associate yourself with your identity. You become a student, I become an engineer.

We associate ourselves with the environmental identity when we are awake. Our consciousness changes when we are sleeping. When we are in deep dreamless sleep, we are at a different consciousness level. When we are half asleep, then we are in a subconscious state. There is a relation between consciousness and our identity.

The identity that we assume in this world is associated with our body or ego consciousness. But is that our real identity? Let's understand that.

Yesterday we spoke about delusion. Do you remember?

Manu: You gave an example of a rope appearing as a snake in the darkness.

Papa: Yes. That is a delusion. Delusion is when we think we are ego but in reality, we are souls.

While being in ego or body consciousness, our senses always connect us with the external world. So, our identity comes from the outside. Throughout our lives, we work hard to create our identity aspiring for more money, a bigger house, luxury cars, more recognition, a better name in society, more power, and whatnot. We think that is the goal of our life and we seek happiness in them. This identity is associated with our ego consciousness.

But our true nature is the soul. Though we achieve many things in life and identify ourselves with them, we don't actually bind with them.

All external achievements don't satisfy our soul, they only bring some pleasure to our ego. Precisely because of this reason, even after having many material achievements, we ask questions like what is my purpose in this life? We feel incomplete in our lives and seek something else.

Without realising our soul nature, we try to achieve more and more things from the outside world, hoping that will bring completeness to our lives. Unfortunately, that does not happen. We just violate the hidden rule of our life jigsaw puzzle game and make our lives more and more complicated. This is our ignorance.

However, there is good news also. We have not lost what we actually are. Our real nature remains dormant but is not gone. It's forgotten but not lost and can be reclaimed.

We still possess divine qualities though they don't manifest. Most of the time we live in ego consciousness, but sometimes we change back to soul consciousness. That is why at the core of our hearts we always remain good. If we want, we can reverse this situation.

Suppose a King goes to a slum area and starts living with the poor people and he forgets he is a King. He will think of himself as poor and live a poor man's life. He will forget his royal life. Someone needs to remind him that he is actually a king. We are also like that king.

We came to this world from the divine world but have forgotten our divine nature. So, we need to be reminded of our real identity.

If you keep a bird in a cage for a long time, the bird will think that is how a bird lives. After that even if we free the bird, she will come back to the cage. Our situation has become like that.

Though we are as free and powerful as God, we become limited by our body and senses.

Abdul Kalam realised this truth. He said others might recognise him with his talents, personality, and what he did in his life. We recognise him as the "Missile Man" of India and the most popular President of India. According to him, who he really is can be discovered through deeper questioning and exploration and through a subtle experience when his mind is peaceful. His real identity will be revealed to him when all preconceptions about him are gone.

"Who am I really? Am I so-and-so with a certain past and a certain body and personality and certain roles, talents, weaknesses, dreams, fears and beliefs? Others may define me in these ways, but that is not who I really am. Who I really am can only be discovered through deeper questioning and exploration, and through a subtler experience of that which is beyond all ideas about myself. It can only be revealed when the mind is quiet and no longer telling me who I am. When all the preconceptions about myself are stilled, what remains is who I really am: consciousness, awareness, stillness, presence, peace, love, and the Divine. You are that which is nameless, and yet has been given a thousand names." – Kalam[1]

We are the souls, the pure consciousness, different from our body and all external identifications. This can be realised only when our mind is quiet and not telling who I am.

Achieving real happiness is the ultimate purpose of life. We must realise our true nature to achieve real happiness. The only way to realise our true nature is to free ourselves from delusion or maya. How do we free ourselves from delusion?

As the light can remove the delusion of seeing a rope as a snake, we need the light of knowledge to see who we really are. Spirituality is that Knowledge. Spirituality is the path to this freedom.

We should use our free choice and make spirituality part of our daily life. Then we will be able to free ourselves from delusion and realise our true nature.

Manu: What exactly should we do to know our true nature?

Papa: God is our creator. He is our Father. Like our Father takes care of our needs, God has not left us here to live with problems. He has given us the technique to free ourselves from this delusion.

Yoga is that technique. Yoga means union. Union with God.

By practising yoga, we can realise our soul nature. We can free our soul from the bondage of our body and senses and make it unite with God. That is the sole purpose of yoga.

If you remember, our soul is wrapped inside five sheaths or *koshas* like a very carefully packed birthday gift. We need to reach to the innermost sheath to know our soul. So, we need to open these koshas one by one to reach our souls.

We have also learned how the initial creative force has come down the astral *chakras* and is resting in the coccygeal or *muladhara* as the *Kundalini* force. This *Kundalini* force should be awakened to move up the astral body.

And finally, the soul consciousness that has descended down the causal body to become body consciousness should move up and become soul consciousness again.

Yoga is a technique to achieve this. It is a scientific technique, a step-by-step approach, following which all the above can be achieved. Just sitting in a quiet place is not meditation or just doing a lot of physical postures is also not yoga.

If this scientific technique is practised correctly and dedicatedly, we all can realise our true divine nature.

Manu: Can you tell me more about yoga?

Papa: There are different forms of yoga.

One of the common forms of yoga that many of us are familiar with is working on different body postures. This is called Hatha Yoga. Hatha Yoga helps to prepare our body for other forms of Yoga.

Karma Yoga, Bhakti Yoga and Jnana Yoga are three other forms of yoga. Karma yoga is union with God through good and right work without any attachment to the work. Bhakti yoga is union with God through devotion. Jnana yoga is union with God through wisdom.

However, the supreme form of yoga is called Raja Yoga, the "royal" yoga. There are multiple scientific techniques of Raja Yoga. Kriya yoga is a technique of Raja Yoga.

Yoga is a science of uniting with God. The ultimate goal of yoga is to free ourselves from the delusion and realise our true nature. We will be able to know God personally if we practice the correct yoga techniques regularly and dedicatedly.

Manu: Will you teach me yoga?

Papa: We should learn yoga from a qualified teacher or "guru". That is very important. Reading from books, learning from videos or even learning from someone who is not qualified may not be very effective.

Right techniques are very important.

A qualified guru does not necessarily always teach us in the normal way of teaching through lectures or demonstrations. A guru can teach us even when he is not near us physically. A God-realised guru has more capabilities to teach us that others cannot do. So in my opinion, to get the true benefit of yoga, we should always learn from a qualified guru.

I am a student now. I still have a lot to learn and practice before I achieve the supreme goal of yoga. I will guide you to the right place, but I am not suitable to teach you the yoga techniques.

However, we can discuss some of the concepts of yoga. When you are studying science, you try to understand the concepts first. Yoga is a science. We can understand the concepts behind Yoga science.

Earlier we discussed three methods of learning. Perception and Inference depend on our senses and intelligence. Intuition is a more powerful method where we can realise knowledge from within. Knowledge in the religious scriptures, the truths about our lives, are realised using our intuitive ability.

The concepts of yoga are also like that. Those who have experienced them through developed intuition after many years of dedicated practice appreciate these concepts better than those who learn them by reading. Whatever I am telling you is primarily from reading and little experience. Though I am practising yoga, I still need time to come to a level where I can completely experience these truths myself. But I have faith that one day I will be able to realise the goal of yoga which is knowing God personally.

I could have asked you to read some books written by a saint or swami who has achieved God-realisation. But you will find it difficult to understand those books at this age. Those books are generally written for adults and will be difficult for children to understand. When you grow big, you should read those books written by God-realised saints and understand more. That knowledge is more pure and authentic as the author attunes to God and writes the facts.

I have read Bhagavad Gita written by Paramahansa Yogananda. In that book, he said that he could understand the spiritual knowledge in Gita by becoming Arjun's soul and talking to God. This is not his interpretation, but what he perceived God telling Arjun by listening through Arjun's intuition. [2]

Only those who have realised God can commune with God. That information is more authentic. When we read them and try to understand them intellectually, we will not appreciate them completely due to our sense limitations.

But, if we practise yoga regularly, our intuition will develop. With developed intuition, we will appreciate these facts better.

You can visualise how you will feel on a snow-covered mountain peak, but you can experience it only when you are there. With intuition, we can experience the divine world.

However, it is important that you understand some basic concepts of spirituality now. This will help you to see religion and spirituality from the right perspective. We often understand them in the wrong way. Gradually you can make spirituality part of your day-to-day life. When you are big, you should read more books and learn from them.

Manu: Sure. I want to be more regular in my meditation practices.

Papa: Let's understand some more concepts of yoga.

Yoga is about transcending our consciousness level. What are these different consciousness levels? Last few days we discussed consciousness in different contexts.

Consciousness is awareness of our existence. The consciousness of our body, senses and external world is what we are aware of in our wakeful hours. In our waking time, mostly we think about things which are external, what we generally perceive through our senses. This is our body or ego consciousness.

When we sleep, we are either in a subconscious state where we are seeing dreams or we are in a dreamless sound sleeping state. They are actually two different levels of consciousness, different from body consciousness.

In the subconscious state or in dreams we do things that we cannot do in our wakeful state. We have an idea of what we experience in the subconscious state as generally, we remember the dream for some time. But we have no idea what we experience in deep dreamless sleep. Actually, our consciousness transcends to soul consciousness in the dreamless sleeping state. This is our natural state.

Soul consciousness is a divine state as it originates from God's consciousness. So everyday night we become divine, but we don't realize it. By practising yoga, we can transcend to this state consciously. This is the power of yoga.

Through the deep practice of yoga, it is possible to expand our consciousness further and realize the entire universe. The universe is finite though we cannot visualise the entire universe with our senses. Our consciousness can cross this boundary of the universe and become infinite to know what is there beyond the Universe. Consciousness beyond the creation is Cosmic Consciousness or God Consciousness. It is possible to transcend our consciousness to the Cosmic Consciousness level. That means we can see the Universe the way God sees it. This is how we can realize God personally.

Realising God is not theoretical, it is a real experience. Ancient yogis could reach this level and advanced yogis could stay in this state in the normal wakeful state also. Realising Cosmic Consciousness, they could hear the cosmic voice intuitively and gain the cosmic knowledge which is there in the scriptures.

Abdul Kalam also realised that there is a fourth level of consciousness and our consciousness can transcend to Cosmic Consciousness. He said,

"I realised that there is a fourth level of consciousness, wherein the consciousness of the self is transcended and becomes cosmic consciousness." [1]

Manu: Wow, we can know God personally!! Sounds impossible to me. How does that happen?

Papa: Yes. It sounds impossible that we can become like God. This is because we think God is separate from us. This is our ignorance. Actually, we need not be surprised. That is our true nature. Returning back to our true nature is not surprising, it is natural. Those who have achieved this are not supermen, they are normal. And those who are not able to achieve this are not realising their potential.

It is like the king who thought he belonged to the slum finds the royal life too high for him. But when he remembers that actually, he was a king earlier, he will not think like that anymore.

There are common people across the world who talk about some kind of enlightenment or awakening that they have experienced suddenly. During this enlightenment or awakening, they feel they are more at peace or calm, in harmony with nature and they lose sense of time and space. This is an expansion of their awareness or in other words elevation of their consciousness from limited body consciousness to a higher level of consciousness. By practising yoga, we can achieve that in a more systematic way.

Soul is our true nature and we can realize our true nature by following the right techniques of yoga.

Manu: What are those right techniques?

Papa: We will not discuss that here. As I told you before, you should learn it from a qualified guru. A qualified guru can teach us the right techniques. But we can try to briefly understand the science behind it.

The ancient sage of India, Patanjali, defined an eightfold path of yoga. They are also called the eight limbs of yoga. Let's try to understand the fundamentals of these eight limbs of yoga.

The great Sage of India, Patanjali, defined eight limbs of Yoga.

The first two stages of the eightfold path are *yama* (abstinence) and *niyama* (observance). They define what we should not be doing and what we should be doing. They are the foundation of spiritual life. For example, we should not cause harm to others and we should be devoted and honest. They are essential at any point of time in our life.

The next stage, *asana,* is about the right posture. Yoga involves working with the life forces inside our body. Right posture helps in easy movement of the life forces. These three limbs are the foundation. They are necessary for the later phases.

Pranayama or breath control is one of the most important limbs of yoga. Pranayama prepares our mind to meditate. Without Pranayama, we cannot do the next steps. When we are able to do *Pranayama* techniques correctly, our mind will reach a state called *Pratyahara* where we are disconnected from our senses.

Concentration is key to mediate. Without achieving concentration, we cannot meditate. However, only concentration is not meditation. Concentration on God is meditation. First, we develop our ability to concentrate and then we meditate on God.

Our senses are the main distraction for us to concentrate.

Suppose you try to focus on your studies and hear some sound. Your mind will go to the source of the sound. For example, you heard some song playing. Your mind will go away from what you are trying to concentrate on and think about the song. What will happen next?

Manu: Maybe I will think from where the song is coming, do I know that song or do I like that song?

Papa: Exactly. And suppose you like the song. Then you might think do you have that with you? When did you last hear that song? Who was with you at that time? Where is that person now? And so on. That is the nature of our minds.

It will pick up something and then follow a chain of thoughts. And we will be in that loop of thoughts before we realize that we deviated from what we were trying to concentrate on. Then we will try to go back to our original focus. It will not be long before we again drift away from that.

Gautam Buddha said our mind is like a fish picked up from the water and kept on the land. Have you seen what the fish will do? It will jump all around. In yoga, we work to control this mind.

Senses are the main cause of distraction. Disconnecting our mind from the senses is key to achieving concentration.

What happens when we are in deep sleep? Our mind is disconnected from the senses. That is why we don't hear any sound and don't feel a touch. This happens unconsciously. In Pranayama we can achieve the same consciously. How does that happen?

Our senses work because of the life force. If the life force or prana does not reach our senses then our senses will be disconnected from our mind. Life forces reach to the senses through the heart. So, the heart needs to stop. That is why pranayama is about breath control. By controlling the breath, the heart can be stopped or slowed down and the senses can be disconnected from our mind.

But, we don't stop the breath forcefully. Some people teach that way but that is not the correct way. In fact, that is harmful. That is why we should learn from a qualified guru.

As we discussed yesterday while trying to understand how our body works so smartly, we learned that breathing happens due to the life force working in our energy body. By consciously controlling this life force, we control our breath. That is why Pranayama is actually life force control.

If you remember the birthday gift example, we are slowly unwrapping the gift and becoming aware of the inner covers. Pranayama makes us aware of life sheath.

Manu: Will we not die if the heart stops?

Papa: Now you can understand why yoga is a science.

Yes, if the heart stops the person will die. But, if the same function that the heart does can be achieved by some other means, then breathlessness is possible when the person is still alive. That is what happens in Pranayama.

What are the main functions of the heart? The main functions of the heart are to pump oxygenated blood to different parts of the body and pump deoxygenated blood with carbon dioxide to the lungs. Oxygen in the inhaled air is transferred to the blood in the lungs and then the oxygenated blood is pumped to the body parts where metabolism happens. Similarly, carbon dioxide, the waste produced during metabolism, is exchanged with oxygen from the blood. The heart pumps this deoxygenated blood with carbon dioxide to the lungs. When we exhale, the carbon dioxide goes out of our body.

The body cells use oxygen to digest the food that we eat and convert it to energy. This is metabolism. The energy produced in metabolism is essential for us to survive. If our body can get the same energy by some other means, then we don't need to depend on breathing. If you remember, the source of all energy is the subtle vibration emanating from Cosmic Consciousness. There is an infinite amount of life energy available in the universe in the form of Cosmic Energy. During the correct practice of the Pranayama technique, our body can draw more life energy from the Infinite source to our body. So, we don't need to depend on breathing and metabolism.

"By deeper Kriya Yoga the bodily life, ordinarily dependent on reinforcement by life force distilled from gross outer sources, begins to be sustained by the cosmic life only; then breathing (inhalation and exhalation) ceases." We can learn this from Bhagavad Gita. *[2]*

Kriya yoga is a pranayama technique. By the deep practice of Kriya Yoga, our body which is generally dependent on outside food can be sustained by the life force available in the cosmos, making breathing unnecessary for survival.

During the practice of Pranayama, as the heart stops or slows down, the mind disconnects from the senses. The mind becomes free from distractions and ready to concentrate. This is the outcome of Pranayama. This state of mind, when disconnected from sense distractions, is called Pratyahara or sense withdrawal.

Manu: Wow!! It is unbelievable. Our hearts can stop and still, we can stay alive.

Papa: Yes. It is true and it is scientific. And that is why we hear many stories of rishis who can live a long time without breathing.

In fact, not only breathing, but one can live without eating also for a long time due to the same reason. Following the Pranayama technique, the body can absorb more life energy from the Infinite Source of Cosmic Energy and energise the cells so that they do not depend on energy from food and oxygen. They can achieve that by following proper scientific techniques.

The next three steps after Pratyahara are "*Dharana*" or concentration, "*Dhyana*" or meditation, and "*Samadhi*" or union.

In *Dharana*, we concentrate on one object and achieve single pointedness. In *Dyana* or meditation, the object of concentration is God. We can concentrate on God or any of His manifestations.

As God is Infinite Consciousness, it is difficult to concentrate on something that does not have any form or shape. God has different manifestations. The astral light or astral sound of 'Aum" is a manifestation of energy coming from Cosmic Consciousness. In meditation, one can see the astral light or hear the astral sound.

We have a third eye called the *Spiritual Eye*. It is there in the middle of our two eyebrows. But we cannot see it in our normal consciousness. As we go deep in meditation, our consciousness changes to a higher state and we will be able to see our spiritual eye.

Through the spiritual eye, we can see a world that consists of subtle energies. This is the spiritual world. The spiritual world is different from our physical world. In the physical world, we see things that consist of gross matter while in the spiritual world, we see things that consist of subtle energies. You don't need your physical eye to see the spiritual world.

As we discussed earlier, our body also consists of subtle energies. In deep meditation, the yogi sees the body as a vibration of subtle energy instead of gross matter.

When we are able to see our spiritual eye and through that the spiritual world, that means we are realising our soul consciousness. We have opened all the layers covering the soul. The *Kundalini Force* that we spoke about earlier has risen up from *muladhara* or coccygeal and reached the astral brain or *sahasrara*. Our consciousness that descended down the causal spine earlier and became body consciousness has moved up the same causal path and became soul consciousness again. This is our true nature. Before we started identifying ourselves with our body and external world, we were the soul knowing the spiritual world. By practising yoga, we can return back to what we were. **This is the meaning of realising our true nature or realising self.**

As we continue to meditate, our consciousness can expand further and know the entire universe. The universe is limited. At the highest level of meditation, called *samadhi or union,* our consciousness will cross the boundary of creation and will become infinite. This infinite consciousness is Cosmic Consciousness or God Consciousness. **This is the meaning of realising God or knowing God personally.**

Samadhi is a blissful state. There is no other experience that can match this state.

By practising the correct techniques of yoga, we can know God ourselves. It is not as simple as I am telling you here, but it is possible. And we all have the inherent potential to know God by ourselves. After all, we are made with the image of Him.

When you finally see the birthday gift wrapped inside many layers of gift wrapping, you feel happy. But after some time, this happiness fades away as your attention will move to something else. What you felt is actually a momentary pleasure. But when you realize your soul and go beyond that to know God personally, what you experience is bliss. This is permanent happiness. This will never fade. **This is the meaning of realising our true nature to be really happy in life.**

So now you understand what is the meaning of realising our true nature, and how we can experience real happiness when we know our true nature. You also understood what it means when we say we can know God personally. These are real experiences. It is not something we got from somewhere else. It is always within us. Yoga has revealed it to us from within.

"Bliss is not added to your nature; it is merely revealed as your true and natural state, eternal and imperishable." – Ramana Maharishi [12]

This infinite consciousness or blissful state is the Absolute. This is the only reality or existence. It is a state of complete freedom without any bondage. And this is our natural state. Within us, we are always in this state. **This is the meaning of you are free.**

Anyone can experience this Absolute. This choice is ours. We are free to decide.

Whenever we have some problem, we pray to God. We ask so many things from God. But when we know God ourselves, we have everything. Then we realize the worthlessness of all the material things that we seek in our entire life. **Knowing God personally is our supreme goal.** No other desire can be higher than that. That is why I said we are not giving up our desires, we are transcending our desires to a higher level.

When we realise our soul, we are free from delusion. We don't see ourselves as mere body or ego. The rope appears as a rope now, not as a snake. We also realize we are not just the limited waveforms, but we are the powerful cosmic sea. The bird locked inside the cage now realises that she belongs to the sky. The king living in the slums as a poor person returns to the royal home.

Search for this bliss makes us feel incomplete. This is the reason for that emptiness or void within us, in spite of many other accomplishments in life.

Now we understand why no material thing can give us the same happiness. Real happiness comes from within, it is not there outside. That is why, in spite of achieving many things in our lives, at some point in time, we feel a kind of emptiness within us. Only by knowing our true nature can we fulfil that emptiness. This is how we can get that mandatory piece of the life jigsaw puzzle game. Yoga is the path to this happiness.

If you stay away from home, initially you may like it, but after some time, you want to come back home. Even if there are many things that you like when you are away from home, they cannot satisfy you fully. You feel something is missing. Only returning home can fulfil that missing feeling. This is a similar feeling. We are away from our real home. Nothing else in this world can satisfy us except for going back to our real home.

You can understand now that we are living in a temporary world. Our identity in this temporary world is also temporary. Like the sea waves, they can disappear at any time. That is why it is not wise to spend our life trying to make this temporary identity.

The eternal purpose and meaning of our lives are to work for the supreme goal of returning to our own self or knowing God.

If we spend our entire lives satisfying our material desires, that is not going to fulfil our eternal purpose. And we will keep coming to this world again and again to learn. But if we work to fulfil our supreme desire to know God, then we can free ourselves from all bindings of karma. Those who can achieve samadhi are free from all karma and need not come back to earth again.

I hope this gives you an idea of what you should do when you grow up. Without realising these truths, if I had answered your question about what you should do when you grow up, you would not have appreciated that so much. But now you understand the truths of life and know the path to happiness.

Manu: But generally, we don't think yoga is mandatory for all. If we want to improve our concentration we meditate. Also, we practice yoga for good health. Those rishis who leave their home and stay in ashrams or mountains probably do more serious yoga as you have explained.

Papa: This is what generally we all think. But this is not true.

The supreme goal of yoga is knowing our true nature and experiencing bliss.

Yoga means union with God.

If we want to experience real happiness, meditation is mandatory. We don't need to go to the mountains to meditate and know ourselves. Anyone can do it anywhere.

Great sage Ramana Maharishi said, *"The one obstacle is the mind; it must be overcome whether in the home or in the forest. If you can do it in the forest, why not at home? Therefore, why change the environment?" [12]*

The mind is the main obstacle in meditation. We need to free our minds from all distractions. Yoga is the scientific technique to achieve that. It does not matter whether we are in the city or the forest.

There are many establishments that help us to learn yoga. We should remember two things.

First, we should learn from a qualified guru. They have higher capabilities to teach what others cannot do. If your guru is God realised, that is the best. In fact, only someone who knows God personally can teach you how to realize God. It is not necessary that your guru is physically around you. They can commune even if they are not around in this physical world.

Second, we should remember the ultimate goal of yoga which is God realisation or knowing God personally. Then only we can experience bliss or real happiness. All other benefits like concentration, health, stress relief or anything else are intermediate benefits. They are useful but not the supreme goal of yoga. Once we know God, everything else we can get. If we are spending our time only to meet the intermediate goals, then we not using our potential fully.

It is also God's desire that we all practice meditation and free ourselves from delusion. I will tell you one true story about how God is trying to help us.

Manu: Yes. I like to listen to stories.

Papa: I have read this in the book *"Autobiography of a Yogi"* by Paramahansa Yogananda. I will tell you briefly. Later you should read that book.

Manu: *"Autobiography of a Yogi"* seems to be your favourite book!!

Papa: Yes. This book has changed my life.

After reading this book I have realised that spirituality is for everyone, not just for those who give up their family and live an ashram life. Working people like me or students like you, everyone should practice spirituality.

Though God has given us free choice to decide, in my opinion, knowledge, and practice of spirituality are mandatory in our lives if we want real happiness. Also, the practice of spirituality is not something we do when we want to or on some special occasion, but it should be part of our everyday life.

After reading this book, at least intellectually, I have understood the purpose and meaning of my life and how to achieve it. I realised the hidden rule of the life jigsaw puzzle game and I know how I can get that mandatory piece to complete my life puzzle. It needs time, dedication, perseverance, and practice. I am into it and I believe, by the grace of my guru and God, that one day I can achieve my goal.

To me, this realisation has come at this stage of my life. I think this is very late. I am fortunate that I decided to spend some time thinking and learning about it. That is how this realisation has come to me. Otherwise, I would have continued to live a purposeless life. It is not that what I have been doing till now was not good, but they were transactional without a purpose. They are required but they are not sufficient to fulfil my eternal purpose of life. They cannot fill the void within me. Now also I do all the material things that I used to do earlier, but I have learned to look at them differently. And I have found more time to meditate and learn spirituality.

Right work in the right way and regular practice of the correct techniques of yoga are required to meet my life's goal. This is my realisation.

This is the reason why I am spending so much time talking to you so that you understand what is the purpose of life and how to achieve it. That will help you to decide what you should do when you grow up.

Yoga is the path to happiness. But only yoga is not enough. We also need to do something else in life. We need to do the right work in the right way. We will talk about it a little later. But now first let me tell you the story.

Manu: Yes, please. I almost forgot about the story.

Papa: Lahiri Mahasaya was the guru of Swami Yukteshswar. Swami Yukteswar was the guru of Paramahansa Yogananda. Lahiri Mahasaya worked for the Military Engineering Department under British rule. In 1861 he was transferred to a place called Ranikhet, currently in Uttarakhand. He was married at that time and he had two sons and two daughters. He was like any other family man.

When he went to Ranikhet, something very exciting happened. One day when he was walking near the forest area, he heard someone calling his name from the forest. When he went there, he found a young man standing near a cave to welcome him. This young man was Babaji, an Indian yogi who is considered to be a Mahavatar.

Babaji took Lahiri Mahasaya inside the cave and pointed at a blanket in the corner of the room and asked him if he remembered the blanket. Lahiri Mahasaya was surprised and said he did not remember. Then Babaji softly touched Lahiri Mahasya's forehead. In a moment everything changed. Lahiri Mahasaya remembered that he and Babaji used to live together in the same cave in the previous life and the blanket was his seat for meditation.

That day night, in the same place where the cave was there, Babaji constructed a big palace for Lahiri Mahasaya. He could do that using his spiritual power. Remember, earlier I told you that all matter is energy, and with our willpower, we can change the form of this energy. That is how God has created the Universe. Babaji has that kind of spiritual power.

Manu: Why did Babaji create the palace?

Papa: It seems, Lahiri Mahasaya had the desire to stay in a palace and Babaji wanted to fulfil that desire. Babaji created the palace for him. Later, inside that palace, Babaji gave initiation to Lahiri Mahasaya. What this means is that Lahiri Mahasaya's consciousness transcended to the Cosmic Consciousness level. Lahiri Mahasaya achieved the state of samadhi. Later Babaji destroyed the palace.

Staying in the state of samadhi for a few days, Lahiri Mahasaya did not want to return back. He requested Babaji to keep him with him. However, Babaji did not agree to that. To this what Babaji replied makes us understand the actual purpose of this incident.

Babaji told Lahiri Mahasaya that he has a responsibility to teach yoga to the household people. Babaji wanted Lahiri Mahasaya to be a role model to the people of the world showing how one can live a balanced life of family, business, and spirituality.

He said, *"Now you are a married man, with modest family and business responsibilities. You must put aside your thoughts of joining our secret band in the Himalayas. Your life lies amid the city crowds, serving as an example of the ideal yogi-householder" [11].*

It is a real story. The important message from this story is that we need not leave our families and jobs to practice spirituality. While doing our jobs and living with our family, we can make spirituality part of our lives. This is a message from God through Babaji who is a Mahavatar. Even the Bhagavad Gita and other religious scriptures teach us the same truth.

You can read the entire story in the "Autobiography of a Yogi" book. There are other interesting true stories in that book.

The reason why Paramahansa Yoganandaji wrote that book and went to the US to teach yoga in the West is a motivational real story for all of us to make spirituality part of our lives. Today many people in the US, India, and other countries are learning yoga.

We should not forget the true purpose of yoga which is God realisation.

Manu: In our school, we also have yoga classes. Now I can appreciate the purpose of yoga better.

Papa: True. It is important for us to practice the right technique of yoga every day. It will not happen overnight. We will have to persevere for a long time.

We should realise that yoga is a science. When we put water in the freezer, it will become ice. That is a scientific process. In the same way, if we practice the correct yoga techniques dedicatedly, we can know God personally. Both are equally scientific.

Yoga is the path to real happiness. We need to choose this path early in our lives.

Tomorrow morning, we need to do our meditation and it is already midnight. We need to sleep now. Good night.

Manu: Oh! We are late again. Good night.

* * *

• 5 •

War of Life

Papa: You seemed sad today. What happened?

Manu: Nothing. I am fine.

Papa: You can tell me. Something might have happened that is making you feel sad.

Manu: Yes. I had a fight with my friend today when we went out to play.

Papa: Oh! Why did you fight?

Manu: It was my mistake also. I wanted to go cycling, but my friend wanted to play inside. But I insisted as yesterday also we were playing inside. Then we got into a small argument. I got angry and I spoke badly to my friend. Then I left.

Papa: Oh! Are you feeling sad because you spoke badly to your friend?

Manu: Yes. Out of anger I told her something and left. Now I regret what I did. I should not have behaved like that.

Papa: This happens to many of us. Often, we lose control of our emotions and later we regret it. Anger is a great enemy of us.

Manu: What do you mean?

Papa: What I mean is anger is not good for us. It is like an enemy for us. We don't want anger. But still, anger will come and do something bad to us.

Manu: Yes. When I get angry, I do something and later I regret it. At that moment it is difficult to control.

Papa: But why do you feel sad after that?

Manu: Because I did not want to hurt her. I want to be good with her.

Papa: Do you realize that you are in a war within yourself?

Manu: How?

Papa: What has happened to you now is a conflict within you.

It is a war between good and bad. You want to be good and don't want to fight with your friend. But then you lose your temper and say something bad to your friend. So, there is a conflict between your wish to remain good and actually behaving differently.

This is an internal war and your anger has won the war today. You could not keep it in your control.

Manu: Yes. At that time, it was very difficult to control my anger, but now I think I should not have done that.

Papa: This is not the only situation and anger is not the only enemy. There are many situations like this and there are many more enemies.

And it is not only you. Everyone engages in this internal war between good and bad.

When you need to study but want to play, you get into an internal war within yourself to control your desire to play and to focus on studying.

When morning I ask you to wake up, but you want to sleep a little bit more, you get into a war within yourself to decide on getting up early and doing something useful or take comfort in sleeping for some more time.

When you are having a cold, but you are near the ice cream shop, you fight to resist your temptations to eat ice cream.

These are a few examples of when you are young. But as you grow big, there will be more good and bad forces working within you and you will be continuously fighting this war.

You may have some bad friends who want to do something bad to have fun. You have to fight against your temptations to go with them and have fun or control your desire not to do that.

You want to help someone with your time or money and at the same time, you want to use your time or money for something beneficial to you.

You want to work hard to earn more money but at the same time, you want to give more time to your family.

Later when you are working, someone offers you a big personal benefit in return for some favour.

Even small things in life like you are driving and there is no one at the red signal at night, you think you should jump the signal or wait; you have the opportunity to use your office vehicle for a personal purpose, should you use it or not; a shopkeeper returns more money to you by mistake, do you return the extra money or keep quiet.

You face many conflicting priorities in your life and get into an internal war within yourself.

Manu: I never realised that. But yes, I think many times I have these conflicting thoughts. One day in class, one of my friends damaged the digital board in the classroom. Later when the teacher asked us to tell who did it, I was in a dilemma whether I should tell or not.

Papa: We all are fighting these internal wars every day without being aware of it. But the results of these internal wars are very important.

Depending on who wins the war determines what kind of person we are. What is our character, and our personality depends on the results of these continuous internal wars.

Manu: Can you tell me more?

Papa: For example, I ask you to wake up in the morning but you want to sleep for some more time. So, you engage in a war between your desire to get up early and do something or surrender to your laziness. If you win the war to get up early and do it regularly, you will become more active and disciplined. Also, you will have more time to do things that you want to do. On the other hand, if your laziness wins the fight, you will sleep more. You will become a lazy person.

Similarly, if you lose the war between your self-control and the temptation of joining your friends, planning something that is not good but fun, you will develop that habit. If your self-control wins the war, you will become a different person.

These small wars within ourselves, between good and bad, are very important in determining what kind of person we are or what kind of person we become.

Manu: How to win these wars?

Papa: We will discuss this. But before that, we need to understand why we have these good and bad things to fight.

Manu: I did not think about that. Can you tell me why?

Papa: You remember we learned delusion. Because of delusion, we don't realize our true nature. Soul consciousness is our true nature, but we think we are ego.

As our true nature is soul consciousness, we have all the divine qualities. By nature, we are calm, pure, truthful, and honest. We have the ability of self-control and self-restraint, we are helpful and compassionate, not greedy, modest and humble, forgiving and patient.

Unfortunately, we have forgotten them and taken up many materialistic qualities due to our ego nature. We have become restless, we don't mind telling lies for our selfish interest, we give up on our temptations very easily, we are selfish and do not care for others, we become angry very quickly, and we are unforgiving and impatient.

When our body is ruled by the soul, we have all the divine qualities. But when the body is ruled by ego, we get all the bodily or materialistic qualities.

The internal war within us is between the soul and the ego and their good and bad forces. Originally the body is ruled by the soul, but the ego has taken control of the body. So, the continuous internal war goes on to take back the lost control.

After doing something bad we regret it. We do bad things under the influence of ego. When the soul gets back the power, we start regretting the bad work. When you were angry you fought with your friend, but later you felt you should not have done that. When you decide to sleep late, you will have a feeling within you that you should get up and do your work. If you decide to be with your friends who are planning something bad for fun, internally you will think maybe I should not have done this. If you lie to someone, you will have guilty feelings within you.

These internal feelings come from our conscience. Conscience says we should wake up early and do some useful work in the morning, don't be in bad company, don't tell lies, and don't be rude to others. Conscience comes intuitively. Intuition connects us with our true nature within.

We have an inherent binding towards all the good qualities but they remain dormant due to overpowering ego.

That is the war of good and bad we are fighting every day within us.

Manu: Some people are good. Some people do many bad things. Why do different people have different characters or personalities then?

Papa: That's a very good question you are asking. Why are we all different?

Not only are we different in character or personality, but we also have many other differences. We are born into different families - some rich, some poor, some Americans, and some Indians. Some people have good health while others have poor health. Someone dies in an accident, and someone else lives a long life.

Many things happen differently to all of us. How is that determined?

We have discussed the Law of Karma. All these differences are governed by the Universal Karmic Law. It is not decided by God. It is decided by us, our actions. Where we are born, how we are today, what is our character, everything is the result of our own actions. The form that we take as humans or something else, the span of life, and the experiences in life are determined by karma.

Our past Karma will decide our environment and our qualities in this life.

The environment includes the family where we are born, health, what kind of people would be around, etc. The qualities determine our character - whether we are good or bad, lazy or active, patient or impatient, selfish or selfless, etc. If you are always angry or fearful in this life and you don't overcome them, these tendencies will appear again in the next life.

We all have an innate nature. Every person has a different innate nature. Innate nature is the natural tendency of our expression.

Some people are by default calm while others are always restless. Some people are always helpful, while others are always selfish. Some people are always active, others are lazy. Some people are in between these extremes. How is our innate nature determined?

Nature is an expression of Cosmic Consciousness. Earlier we spoke about Cosmic Maya or delusion that is required for creation. A storm is needed to form the waves in a calm sea. Similarly, nature manifests from calm Cosmic Consciousness because of the Cosmic Maya or delusion.

All the three gunas are present in us. The dominant guna determines our innate nature.

There are three modes of expression of nature called the gunas or the attributes. They are *sattva*, *rajas* and *tamas*. In the formless or unchanged, these three gunas are in complete balance. That is why God is called *nirguna*. But, in manifestations of Cosmic Consciousness, they are not in balance. All three exist in all manifestations, but one of them will be dominating. They are the positive, neutral, and negative attributes of the subtle current or energy that constitutes nature.

Our body is also part of nature and we also exhibit these three modes of expression.

Sattva means good, rajas means passion or activity and tamas means ignorance. Every person has all three guans, but one of these gunas will be dominant on us based on our past karma. If sattva is the dominant guna on a person, he will be good, high in spirituality, generally will see good things, and guided by wisdom. He will be eager to perform service that is good for all. A rajasic person is active and passionate about the material world. His material desires and selfish motives are stronger. Most of the people in the world are rajasic. A tamasic person will be lazy, more inclined towards bad habits, will generally see the bad in everything, and be ignorant.

Why do different people have different compositions of these three gunas? Why are some people sattvic by default while some other people are tamasic? It is not decided by God, it is decided by our Karma. Let me try to explain.

Assume our mind is like a lake. Our thoughts are like the ripples in the lake. They come, become bigger and then gradually disappear. But actually, they don't disappear completely. They remain as subtle impressions in our subconsciousness and can appear again. These impressions are called the *samskaras.*

Thoughts in our subconscious and conscious minds drive our actions. They are our karma. Our character is nothing but our actions and thoughts. Past karma leaves impressions in our consciousness like the ripples in the lake that do not disappear completely and can come back again. This is how our karma, past or present, defines our character. Each man's character is determined by the sum total of these impressions.

The innate nature of every person is different based on past karma.

Manu: Can you give some examples?

Papa: Sometime back we discussed one situation. When I ask you to wake up in the morning you get into an internal war between your wish to sleep more or your need to wake up early and finish some work. Different people will respond differently to this. If your dominant guna is rajasic, you are an active person. Generally, you will win the war against laziness and you will wake up. On the other hand, if you are a tamasic person, more likely you will give up on your laziness and will sleep more.

You want to help someone needy with your money. But you have some other priority for yourself. If you are rajasic, you are dominated by your personal desires. So, you will mostly decide to fulfil your own needs. If you are sattvic, you will have a stronger desire to help others

These are just a few examples. But over time, in different instances, based on the dominant guna on us, our responses will be different. These responses are our natural tendencies and these natural tendencies build our character.

Manu: I think I am rajasic.

Papa: Yes. Could be.

Most of the people in this world are rajasic - passionate and active but driven by desires to fulfil their own needs.

Manu: I have a doubt now. If it is already decided what kind of person we are, then what is the point of us trying to become better?

Papa: That is a very good point.

But by now you might have realised that the creation and sustenance of this Universe are done in a very intelligent way. There is an Intelligent force working behind everything. There is a reason why things are in a certain way in this universe. It is by design, not random. We learned about Cosmic Intelligence.

The gunas are nature's way of manifesting different qualities in us. But we can change it.

This world is a learning school for us. If we have many negative qualities in us, that means we have not learned enough. We are still living in delusions. We need to learn more and become good. Until the time we don't complete our learning, we need to visit the school. Only by becoming good can we get rid of all bad karma.

We have the free choice to decide and we also have the technique to become good. Yoga is the technique that can change our innate nature. By practising yoga, we can realise our true nature and manifest our divine qualities.

Paramahansa Yoganandaji said, *"Human personality can be changed to divine personality. " [13]*

Every Night, in dreamless sleep, when our consciousness changes to soul consciousness, our personality becomes divine. We can achieve the same in a wakeful state by practising yoga. The choice is ours.

Manu: Can you tell me how to become better?

Papa: What is the meaning of becoming better?

Becoming better means changing our default state of being.

As we have learned, our default state of being is ego. We live in the body consciousness. Our senses connect us to the external world and we display many materialistic qualities. Though we change to soul consciousness occasionally and display good qualities, because of the overpowering ego we cannot remain in that state for a long time. Very easily we get attracted to the material world and our nature changes. This is the war between soul and ego.

If we want to become better, we should make the soul win this war. If the soul controls our body for most of the time, or in other words our consciousness changes to soul consciousness, we will reflect the divine qualities more. That is the meaning of becoming better. On the other hand, if we live in body consciousness for most of the time then we will remain restless, selfish, impatient, unforgiving, and so on.

Yoga is the technique to achieve this. If we practice yoga regularly, we will be more calm than restless, more compassionate than selfish, our self-control will become stronger than our temptations, we will be more forgiving than rude, more patient than short-tempered, more honest and truthful than telling lies to meet our selfish desires, humble and modest than being arrogant, showing more love and care to others instead of ignoring or hurting others. What else do we need?

By helping the soul win the internal war over the ego we can gain back all these divine qualities.

Manu: How exactly does that happen? How yoga can make us better.

Papa: The practice of yoga changes our consciousness from body to soul. That is how the soul can get control of us. But how does it change our personality? Let's understand that.

Ego and Soul are always at war. Good forces of wisdom, discriminative intelligence, intuition, calmness, and self-control fight against the bad forces of ignorance, bad habits, endless desires, and uncontrolled emotions.

There are good and bad forces in our body. The good forces fight for the soul while the bad forces fight for the ego. The result of the internal war between good and bad depends upon which forces are stronger. The good and bad forces are the soldiers fighting for the soul and ego.

Manu: What are those forces?

Papa: The good forces are Wisdom, Discriminative Intelligence, Intuition, Calmness, and Self-control. If these forces are active in our body then they can fight against the bad forces and defeat them.

The bad forces are Ignorance, Endless Desires, Bad Habits, and Uncontrolled Emotions.

With the help of wisdom, discriminative intelligence, intuitive power, and self-control we can overcome our ignorance, strong material desires, bad habits and temptations, anger, and other bad emotions.

If we want the soul to win the internal war, we need to make these good forces stronger. In other words, we need to have access to these good forces easily.

When we get angry and calmness is not around us, anger will win. But if calmness is always around us, anger cannot come. You are tempted to do something bad. If you have access to self-control easily, you will be able to control your temptations. If self-control does not come naturally to you, your temptations will overcome you.

Yoga makes these good forces accessible to us easily.

You remember the birthday gift example. If you need to spend time unwrapping the gift, that means it is not easily available to you. If you have already opened it, it is just beside you. Yoga opens up the *koshas* or the sheaths covering our soul and makes the soul power easily available to us. We learned about it yesterday.

Where are these good forces in our body?

You remember the causal body. These good forces are located in our causal body. The causal brain in our cerebrum is the house of Divine Wisdom, the causal medulla centre is the power of Intuition, the causal cervical centre is our calmness, the causal dorsal centre is the vital power of our life force and the causal lumber is the centre of self-control and the power of adherence and restraint comes from the sacral and coccygeal centre. [2]

By practising yoga, we become aware of our astral and causal body and the good forces manifest in us easily. Our consciousness changes from body to soul. We get access to all the divine qualities.

In other words, regular practice of correct yoga techniques will make us wiser with the divine knowledge gained through our intuition, we will have a higher discriminating ability to decide between good and bad, we will have the ability to remain calm and the strong ability of self-control will help us to win over our mental and physical temptations. All these stronger forces will fight back against the bad forces of desires, habits, emotions, and ignorance.

Abdul Kalam narrated this story to a group of students whom he invited to Rashtrapati Bhavan. *"Remember, there are two people sitting on everyone's shoulders. On the right sits the angel and on the left sits Satan. Every time you do good deeds, the angel wins and every time you do bad deeds Satan wins. Knowledge makes the angel free; it makes him powerful. Ignorance makes Satan free; it makes him powerful.* "[1]

Manu: This is very interesting.

Papa: Now let's see how each of the bad forces can be defeated by the good force.

First, let's take the example of endless material desires. On the first day, we discussed that we go behind endless material desires in pursuit of happiness. But now we have learned that fulfilling material desires cannot give us real happiness. So, it is not worthwhile to spend our life working only for money, name, power, etc. That will not help us to fulfil our eternal goal.

However, there is a difference between working to fulfil our needs and working for the betterment of mankind and working for power, name, money, etc. We need to do our duty but we need to control our desires. It may look like we are giving up happiness. In reality, we are giving up temporary pleasure for real happiness. We are transcending our desires to a higher level. We need intuitive wisdom to realise this truth.

Those who understand realising God as the supreme desire, for them other desires have very little meaning. They don't run behind money, power, name, and fame. They understand our delusive nature and realise our goal is to free ourselves from it.

But many of us have not reached that level yet. We need more time before we can really understand that realising God is our supreme desire. Still, regular practice of yoga will help us to come out of our endless desires.

As we practice yoga regularly and our consciousness starts moving upward, we will get access to our divine qualities residing in our causal body. Our intelligence will become discriminative, we will become more intuitive and self-control will become stronger. Developed intuitive wisdom will tell us the worthlessness of going behind endless material desires. We can use our enhanced discriminative intelligence to judge which desire is good and which desire is not good.

Ask your conscience. Conscience is divine guidance. When your intuition is developed, your conscience will be more accurate. We get direct access to God's guidance in our day-to-day lives. This is how we can come out of the rat race of endless desires.

Slowly we will realize the hidden rule of our life jigsaw puzzle game. By having fewer desires, we can find real happiness. We are trying to solve our life puzzle with a few pieces. This will keep our lives simple and will help us to get that mandatory piece of happiness.

Bad habits are another example of a bad force within us. Let's how we can defeat this enemy of ours.

Nowadays many children get addicted to online games and phone usage. We also hear people getting addicted to different abusive substances. These are examples of habits.

Once we develop a habit, it is very difficult to change. Habits can be good or bad. Good habits are helpful for us. But bad habits are our enemies.

Manu: I always want to sleep late in the morning.

Papa: If you do it regularly that becomes a bad habit.

At a young age, we have a few bad habits. But as we grow up, we may develop more bad habits. And sometimes those habits become so intense within us that we don't find any way to come out of that. They can completely spoil our lives.

Laziness, drinking, gambling, and addiction to online games or other inappropriate content available online are a few examples of bad habits to name which can ruin our lives. How do we control our bad habits?

Primarily we need two abilities to control our bad habits. First, we should be able to discriminate between good and bad, and then we should be able to control our temptations. Yoga enables us with both these abilities.

You want to sleep late because of your laziness. But as you develop your ability to reason out how waking up early can help you, you can overcome laziness. The ability to reason comes with higher intelligence and a calm and clear mind. As your consciousness moves higher through the regular practice of yoga, your intelligence becomes discriminative due to developed intuition and connection with divine wisdom.

You have played a few online games and enjoyed them. You want to play more. That is your temptation. You need stronger self-control to resist that temptation. The causal lumber in our causal body is the power centre of self-control. As you meditate and your consciousness rises, you get access to this power of self-control to overcome your temptations.

There is another force that will work to stop changing our habits. That comes from our past karma. We need to be aware of that force also.

When you try to get up early, thoughts of the comfort of sleeping will come to your mind. That will try to force you to sleep more, even though you reason out that you should get up early. When you are trying to resist the temptation of playing an online game, thoughts of having fun while playing the game will appear in your mind and will try to invite you to play the game.

These thoughts are impressions in our minds from the past. They are the samskaras that we discussed some time back, the ripples in the lake that do not disappear completely and can appear in our conscious or subconscious mind.

Some of these impressions could be from this life and some could be from past lives also. They are our inner tendencies due to past habits - actions or thoughts.

Samskaras will fuel the habits. Good samskaras will help us to develop good habits, but bad samskaras will support bad habits.

In a strict sense, If I say I have control over my habits means I can control both good and bad habits. My ability to control habits is the ability of self-control to stop my temptations. The temptations could be for good or bad. One who has real control over habits can control both good and bad habits. All the good work he does is not because of the influence of the temptation, but because of his wisdom to do good. This is freedom.

Manu: But will it not take some time to develop these good qualities?

Papa: Yes. It will not happen overnight. It will take time and we will start manifesting these divine qualities as we continue to practice meditation.

Manu: Before I develop these qualities if I need to change some bad habits, how do I do that?

Papa: This is a very practical question. It is like the chicken and egg problem. I can give one suggestion.

Generally, temptations will give you some pleasure immediately but in the long term, they will have some bad effects. For example, you like to play online games and you get tempted to play more and more. You enjoy the thrill while playing the game. But you know in the long term it is not good. It might affect your studies and health.

When you come across a temptation like this, first you should say "No", as a rule, and stay away from them even before you try to reason it. Because, if you try to reason it and decide yes or no, most of the time your reason will fail in front of the stronger temptations. The immediate pleasure will force you to decide yes. But once you say no and stay away from the temptation for some time and then try to reason it, your answer will be based on merit. Then your mind is calm and you can use your discriminative intelligence.

So the simple rule is just to say "No" and walk away or divert your mind from the temptation. With meditation, as your self-control and discriminative intelligence will strengthen, you will be able to do it more easily.

Manu: Anger is another big problem. As I told you, because of anger, sometimes I do things that I regret later. How do I control my anger?

Papa: Yes, as we discussed, anger is another big enemy of ours.

Anger is an emotion. It is a feeling.

Anger is a negative emotion. Some emotions are positive while some emotions are negative. Happiness, joy, hope, love, and gratitude are a few examples of positive emotions. Anger, sadness, fear, loneliness, and hate are some examples of negative emotions.

Negative emotions are our enemies. Anger is one of our biggest enemies. You told me you spoke harshly to your friend as you were angry. When we are angry, we lose our ability to think and rationalise and we end up doing something bad. Many crimes happen due to anger.

Even other negative emotions are not good for us. Being sad for a long time can make us depressed. Fear causes stress. Continuous stress will do harm to your body. Fear also affects our performance. You remember how nervous you were in the piano recital when you were performing in front of many people. If you become nervous about the exam, you may forget everything you learned. Continuous stress can bring many serious health issues like diabetes and high blood pressure.

There is much research happening in the area of emotional intelligence these days and they suggest different tools that can help to control our emotions. Like we measure our Intelligent Quotient (IQ), we can measure our Emotional Quotient (EQ) also. Only a higher IQ is not enough. We need higher EQ also to become a balanced person. Many of the tools to improve our emotional intelligence are psychological. They work at the psychological level.

Yoga is a scientific spiritual technique that can help us to control our emotions while working on our spiritual body.

The causal cervical centre in our causal body is the centre of calmness. Through regular practice of yoga, we get access to this divine quality. When calmness becomes our default nature, emotions do not disturb us. We become a calm sea, the restless waves cannot touch us.

Why do you get angry? Have you thought about it for some time?

Manu: When I don't like something, I get angry. Sometimes when someone else does something not as per my wish it makes me angry.

Papa: In other words, when you don't get what you want, you get angry.

You were angry with your friend because she did not want to go cycling. It was your desire that she cycles. When your desire was not fulfilled you got angry.

The root cause of our anger is unfulfilled desire.

Even other negative emotions are also results of our unsatisfied desires. You want your sister to stay with you. When she leaves for the hostel, you feel sad. Your desire to be near your sister is not fulfilled.

As you grow up, you will find many such unfulfilled desires. You want a particular kind of job, but you don't get it. At work, you will not get a promotion or hike what you wanted badly. You thought you did very good work and expected some recognition, but others ignored you. Your spouse or children will not behave the way you want them to behave. While driving, you want all people on the road to follow discipline. They don't. All these unfulfilled expectations will make you angry, sad, frustrated, disappointed

Unsatisfied desire causes negative emotions. When we have few materialistic desires, we will have fewer reasons to be angry, sad, frustrated, or disappointed. As we discussed some time back, yoga will help us to control our desires. Fewer desires mean fewer unhappy moments.

When you get angry, you find it difficult to control your anger. That happens only for a brief period of time. Moments later you will start thinking why did you behave like that? The sense signals are sent to two parts of our brain - one is the emotional part and the other is the rational part. The amygdala is the emotional brain and the neocortex is the rational brain. The sense signals first to reach the Amygdala so that we can respond to an emergency situation quickly. During this brief period of time, our rational brain will not function. The amygdala hijacks our rational brain. That is why when we get angry first, we react and then we think and act.

Research says it takes about six seconds before our rational brain takes over. That means when you get angry if you can control your reaction for about six seconds, you will act instead of reacting. Those six seconds are a very crucial time in managing our emotions.

If you are a person who practices yoga regularly, you have easy access to your self-control in your causal lumber. Self-control will come naturally to you. Your self-control will stop you from reacting. This will give enough time to your rational brain and with developed discriminative intelligence you will respond wisely. That is how one who practices yoga regularly will have a very different behaviour upon getting angry than the one who does not practice yoga.

So you have seen how the good forces of self-control, calmness, and intuitive wisdom help us to fight back against the bad forces of uncontrolled emotion. We get access to these good forces in our causal body as we open up the koshas through the regular practice of yoga.

Manu: After you taught me to practice self-control, I feel I am able to control my anger to some extent, but not always. Now I understand how I can make my self-control stronger by practising yoga regularly.

Papa: Yes. Yoga will make you calm and you will have better self-control. These are divine qualities.

Ignorance is probably the biggest enemy of ours. We face many problems due to our ignorance.

The biggest ignorance is that we don't know our true nature. We live in delusion due to ignorance. Linked with that are all the other negative forces we discussed. Endless material desires, bad habits, and bad emotions are all due to a lack of wisdom.

That there can be wheels to make movement easier is knowledge. Not knowing that wheels can make movement easier is ignorance. Before the invention of the wheel, people lived in ignorance.

Knowing that the soul is our true nature is knowledge. Not knowing our true nature believing that ego is our nature and spending our lives to satisfy ego is our ignorance. Most of us are still living in this ignorance.

Realising that we are ignorant is the first step towards wisdom.

Manu: How to be knowledgeable then?

We go to school and learn. As I understand, almost all people who work in companies, hospitals, banks, schools or do their own business are highly educated people. Then why Ignorance is a reason for many of our problems?

Papa: You are asking a very good question.

Even if we exclude people who live in rural India where the literacy percentage is lower, in the cities most of the people are educated. Then why is ignorance the cause of our problems? I will try to explain it to you.

Let me ask you a very simple question. What do you learn in school?

Manu: We learn many subjects in school. We learn mathematics, science, social science, language, and computers. So many things we learn in school.

Papa: Yes. We learn so many things from school. And because of all the learning from school, we are able to get jobs and do many good things in our lives.

There are many good doctors across the world who have improved the healthcare system significantly. There is so much improvement in Science and Technology and our living has become a lot easier due to the excellent work of Scientists and Engineers from these schools and colleges. With the help of many good teachers, we can learn so much from school. There are many other professionals like lawyers, psychologists, designers, geologists, and many more who get trained in schools and colleges and contribute to their respective domains. School education is the reason for most of the developments we see around us.

The learning in school is to prepare us for the future job.

We study science and know how nature works, we learn history and geography, and in civics, we learn how the government works, learn mathematics, and also learn different languages. Later we learn engineering, medicine, and laws or learn science more deeply when we study pure science. These learnings give us a lot of information and improve our intelligence. We become well-informed and very intelligent.

But we cannot understand life with intelligence. Life is not about reason or logic. Intelligence does not necessarily mean wise. We use our intelligence to achieve our material goals. But can satisfying all those material goals give us happiness? We need wisdom to answer this, not intelligence.

Through yoga, when we develop our intuition, we have access to divine wisdom. Yoga makes us wise. By practising yoga, we will make wise decisions than merely intelligent decisions. Discriminative intelligence is intelligence guided by wisdom. Yoga enhances our discriminative intelligence power. Instead of intelligence, we should use our conscience and intuition for our day-to-day guidance. Conscience and intuition have divine power.

Traditional learning helps us to develop our intelligence. All skills we learn at school make us intelligent but not necessarily wise. The practice of yoga and knowledge of spirituality will make us wise. To live a happy life, we need both.

We need wisdom to use our intelligence in the right way.

In ancient India, students used to study under the guidance of a guru in an ashram. Spiritual teaching and yoga practices were part of that learning besides the skills required for future work. Like we learn different skills in schools these days to do our future job, they also used to learn skills preparing for the future. Taking part in the war was mandatory for them and so they used to learn fighting skills. Along with that, they used to learn spirituality and yoga. So, they were both intelligent and wise.

Unfortunately, nowadays, we focus more on developing only our intelligence. Equipped only with intelligence, as we grow and face the challenges of life, we find ourselves unprepared.

Due to a lack of wisdom, we don't handle our lives properly. We give up our health to achieve more money thinking that will give us happiness. We behave selfishly for our personal growth thinking that is the most important thing in life. We lose our temper and fight with others assuming we are always right. Many live a very insecure life always in the fear of losing something or something bad happening.

If we develop our intuition and listen to our conscience, we will not do many of the things that we are doing otherwise.

Death is our greatest fear. Ignorance is the main reason for this fear of death. We fear losing the physical body and all temporary things around us, including our relations. We don't realize the glorious afterlife in the astral world. This is ignorance. When we die with fear and unfulfilled desire, karmic law makes us come back to earth again. If we overcome the fear of death, knowing the truths of life, we move forward in our eternal goal towards liberation. That is wisdom.

Truths of life and realisation of them are real knowledge. That can give us real happiness. We can know our true nature by knowing the truths of life. Otherwise, we live a delusive life. We don't get this knowledge from school.

We get this knowledge from Spirituality. Without this divine knowledge, we can never understand our life. We will always remain ignorant. This is what I meant when I said Ignorance is the cause of many of our problems, though many of us are highly qualified.

Similar to the Kurukshetra war between good and bad, each person has to fight his own battle of Kurukshetra. We can learn it from the Bhagavad Gita. [2]

All of us need to fight this war of life between good and bad. If we want to win this war, meditation is the only way. Through regular practice of meditation under a qualified guru, we can gain back soul consciousness and all our divine qualities. When we have intuitive wisdom, calmness and the ability of self-control, we can defeat the enemies of desires, bad habits, negative emotions and ignorance.

Manu: How about our other responsibilities and needs? You said we need to do the right work and in the right way. What is my right work?

Papa: Yes. I remember your question - what should you do when you grow up? I have not answered that question till now.

In the last few days, we have understood the truths of our life and we know the path to happiness. Today we have also learned how to win the war of our life.

We spoke about the right work in the right way. What is the right work and what is the right way?

We need to spend some time understanding this. After that, I can answer your question. We are late for today. Let's discuss it tomorrow again.

Manu: Oh! Already very late. Good night.

Papa: Good night.

* * *

• 6 •

Code of Work

Manu: Papa, today we are supposed to discuss what is the right work and what you mean by the right way. I am still looking for the answer to my first question about what I should do when I grow up.

Papa: Yes. Now is the time to answer that question.

Generally, we live a kind of programmed way of life, without thinking about what actually we want in life. It is good that we are discussing this now before you set yourself into that mode of programmed life.

As students, we are busy with studying and playing, some of us also learn music, sports, dance, or other hobbies; then we join work and get busy settling into the new work environment. By the time we settle into a job, marriage happens and the new responsibility of family and raising kids becomes our priority. As we enter middle age, career growth, social status, and taking care of aging parents become our concerns. By the time we are done with all these aspirations and responsibilities, a good part of our life is over.

If you see the schedule of your day, it is mostly preoccupied with already planned activities. Life is just an extension of that. Though there are some exceptions, for most people like us, life follows a pattern like this and we move on keeping ourselves busy in this almost fixed pattern of living.

I don't want to give a very negative picture of our life. There are many positives in the way we live our lives.

Many good things also happen in this automated way of living. We get the occasional pleasure of achieving something important - for example, a good result in an exam, or a promotion in a job; we make many relations, get love and care from people around us; we even get our dream desires satisfied - doing exceptionally well in our career and making lots of money, going on the most exotic vacation, having a very good position in the society and power; and we might even do many social and community services to derive internal satisfaction.

With all these nice things, some painful things also happen to us. We have moments of failure at school or at work that upset us; unsatisfied desires that make us unhappy and sad, sometimes angry, even though many of our other desires are satisfied; there are broken relationships with friends and family members; financial loss or insufficient money to fulfil our basic needs; bad health, death of someone close to us and so on.

If you remember, on the first day we spoke about three types of needs that we have. Physical needs, psychological needs, and spiritual needs. Money and most of the material things satisfy our physical needs. Family, friends, love, and care from people around us, praise and recognition, and satisfaction of doing a good job satisfy our psychological needs. For a good part of our lives, fulfilling these two needs keeps us occupied.

Once we are settled with our physical and psychological needs to a good extent, spiritual needs appear in our lives. At this point in time, we start thinking about the purpose of our life. Why are we here and what are we supposed to do? What is the real meaning of life? We don't find an easy answer to these questions and it leaves us with some kind of empty feeling within.

Spiritual needs arise naturally.

Now we have learned how to satisfy our spiritual needs. We know why we get that empty feeling in spite of fulfilling our physical and psychological needs and what can fill that void. We have understood the truths of life and the path to happiness. We also learned how regular practice of yoga can help to win the war of life.

When you asked me what you should do when you grow up if I had suggested to you some good profession with better opportunities and matching your interests, that would have satisfied your ego, not your soul. Then, at a later stage of your life, once your material and psychological needs are satisfied, you will search for meaning and purpose in your life. By then it becomes too late to ask that question. Now we have preempted that situation.

When we say life, what is the duration of our life - the time from our birth till the time death happens? That is what we understand when we say life. When we are discussing the goal of life, we are thinking about what we want to achieve before our death. However, life from birth to death is the life of the physical body, not of our true self.

As we have learned, our true self is the soul. The life of the soul is much longer than the life of the physical body.

If we just think about the goal of our life within the span of physical life, that would be short-term thinking. If we have understood life correctly, as taught by our religions, then the purpose of this life is not just what we do in the physical span of life, but what we want to achieve in the eternal span of our life.

The supreme goal of knowing God is an eternal goal. The progress we make in every physical lifespan towards the goal of God-realisation is positive progress toward the eternal goal. We may achieve it in one life or in multiple incarnations. But we are moving towards the supreme goal. We need to remember this truth.

Manu: Still, we will have other responsibilities in life. We need money to live. We need to work to fulfil those responsibilities.

Papa: You are absolutely right. As we grow big, we need to take up some profession.

We have our basic necessities in life. In order to fulfil our basic necessities, we need money. We need food to survive, we need a comfortable life, we need to take care of our health, and we need to take care of our dependent family members. So, we need to work on something so that we can earn money and take care of our basic needs.

However, working to only fulfil our basic needs is not enough. Mankind would not have developed so much if everyone worked only to fulfil their basic needs. It is because of the contributions of all people that the human race is developing continuously. We all need to work towards the development of mankind.

Fighting the Kurukshetra war was Arjuna's duty. Serving a sick patient is the duty of a doctor. Teaching a student is the duty of a teacher. Making human living easier is the duty of the technologist. A farmer makes food available to all of us. Even a cleaner in a public place is serving people. Each profession is serving mankind. Every person has some duty towards the development of human society. This is the right work that I mentioned earlier.

Our duty towards the development of mankind is the right work or rightful duty for us.

Basic needs and rightful duties are the two optimal pieces that we need to complete the life jigsaw puzzle game.

Basic needs and rightful duties are two other puzzle pieces that are needed in our jigsaw puzzle game of life. They are those optimal numbers which are required to complete the game along with the mandatory piece of happiness. But when we try to have more than this optimal number while trying to get more money than required, more luxury than what is essential, social power and status to satisfy our ego and so on, then the puzzle becomes more complex and it becomes almost impossible for us to get that mandatory piece of happiness. **This is the hidden rule of the life jigsaw puzzle game.**

Manu: How do I know what is the right work for me?

Papa: If you think about all the people in the world, everyone is doing different work. But as a result of all the work done by different people in different parts of the world, there are so many developments happening in this world. The human race is progressing because of all the good work done by people like all of us. Is it happening randomly or is there some intelligence behind it? Let's understand this.

What decides what work you do?

The environment where we live and our nature are the two fundamental factors that determine what work we do in our lives. The environment determines the opportunities that we get in life. Depending on our family background, the place where we live and our interest decides what education we get and what skills we learn. And that will determine what profession we take.

For example, two persons living in two different parts of the world, even though they have the same interests and skills could be doing different work based on the opportunities available. Two persons living in the same part of the world could be doing different work depending on interests and skills.

Both the environment where we live and our nature are the results of our past karma. Whether we are born in the East or West, rich or poor, to an educated or uneducated family, healthy or unhealthy etc. is determined by our past karma. Similarly, whether we are a Sattvic, Rajasic or Tamasic person is based on the dominant guna. The dominant guna is again determined by our past karma.

There is a Cosmic Influence on what we are today.

We are assigned a role to perform in the Cosmic plan of God. We need to perform that role. This is our rightful duty. Not doing our rightful duty will influence the cosmic plan and it will affect our karma.

In Mahabharata, Arjuna did not want to fight the war against his relatives and gurus. But defeating the bad forces, represented by the kurus, was his rightful duty. Denying to fight due to attachment with the kurus will be selfish. In the Bhagavad Gita, Krishna makes Arjuna understand that no one can escape "*swa-dharma*" or rightful duty. Arjuna is a "*Kshatriya*" and his job is to fight the war.

Like Arjuna, we all have our *"swa-dharma" or* rightful duty and we need to fulfil that.

Depending on the environment we live in and our skills and interests, any work that is good for the development of mankind is a rightful duty.

Most of the work that people are doing around us - teaching, medicine, engineering, entrepreneurship, and farming all are rightful duties. I remember we studied complementary skills in your Social Science book. You understand why complementary skills are required for better living and development.

Not all work is rightful duty. Only those works that serve the development of mankind are rightful duty. For example, stealing, immoral ways of making money, and making or selling prohibited products are definitely not rightful duties.

These are just examples. We need to use our discriminative intelligence to judge if we are doing our rightful duty. This ability comes with the practice of yoga.

Abdul Kalam said it very beautifully. He said, *"It is my belief that a person's conscience develops at the pace at which his relationship with God develops. And as both develop, the inner voice—which is available to us all—becomes stronger and more reliable as a guide for the actions one plans."* [1]

Kalam believed that our inner conscience is a reliable guide for the actions that we plan in our lives. As we develop our relations with God, our conscience also develops.

So don't worry about whether you know your rightful duty or not. Whatever good work comes to you, think of it as your duty. Not every work comes to everyone. There is an intelligent system working behind it. If you have any doubt, ask your conscience. God will guide you through your conscience. Develop your intuition through the regular practice of yoga to hear the divine guidance in everyday life.

Manu: You said right work in the right way. What do you mean by the right way of doing the right work?

Papa: Let me ask you a simple question. For whom will you do the rightful duty?

Manu: Is it not for myself?

Papa: That is where we can go wrong again.

If I am doing something for my benefit, that means I have a selfish desire.

When a doctor treats a patient for whom does he work? For the patient or for himself.

Manu: Maybe for both. The doctor will get money and the patient will get treatment.

Papa: True. But there is a subtle difference.

If the primary motive of the doctor is making money, then his actions can be different. He will be inclined to do things that can help him to make more money. Definitely, he will fight the internal war that we spoke about yesterday. His conscience will try to stop him from doing something wrong. But if his conscience is not developed and he thinks material achievement is the goal of life, then he will not mind doing things that help him to earn more money but may not be required for the benefit of the patient. Though he is doing the right dutiful work, he is not doing it in the right way. Such stories are not uncommon in our society.

The intention with what we do our rightful duty is important. That will decide our exact actions.

If we are still living in delusion, then we will work to make our identity around many material things. If we have not understood the hidden rules of the life jigsaw puzzle game, we will try to acquire more puzzle pieces available to us thinking that will give us happiness. That is how we become selfish. Though we are doing the rightful duty, we will have our selfish interest in it.

A rightful duty is for the betterment of mankind. Not to fulfil our own desires. Performing our rightful duty with an attachment will not serve the cosmic plan. It will affect our karma.

The universal law of karma recommends *"nishkama karma"* or "*selfless seva*". Work for the sake of work without any motives. Don't have any attachment to the fruits of your work.

Non-attachment to the fruits of our work will make us selfless. We will do our work as a service to mankind and fulfil the divine plan. This is what I said earlier as the right way.

We need to do the right work in the right way. That is the code of work.

Manu: What is the motivation then? If we don't expect any benefits from our work, what will motivate us to perform?

Papa: You are right. Our intelligent mind may not find any motivation to do any work if there is no gain from it.

When we are bound by material desires and working to fulfil them, we will evaluate every opportunity with the question, *"What is in it for me?"* We don't want to do anything if it does not help us reach our goals.

But we don't understand the purpose of our life. So obviously we cannot evaluate how selflessness can help us to achieve our life goals. This is our ignorance.

If we know the truths of life, as taught by our religious scriptures, and realize them, then we understand the purpose of our life. Then we will know how selflessness can help us to achieve our life goals. When we realize this, we will see every work opportunity as a service to mankind. We will understand our role in the divine plan. Doing our part of work as per the divine plan is a step forward towards our supreme goal of achieving real happiness and knowing God.

The goal of our lives can be transcended from desiring momentary pleasure through material things to achieving real happiness through seeking God.

So, we are still working to fulfil our own goal. The difference is, that we are not working to fulfil the material goal of this life, instead, we are working to fulfil the supreme goal of our eternal life. This is what I meant by transcending our desires to a higher level.

It will take time to realize this. As long as we live in delusion, we are bound by material desires. We cannot do selfless service. As we learn more about spirituality and practice yoga, we will become wiser and our discriminative intelligence will improve. Then we will understand what is our supreme goal and gradually we will learn to do selfless service.

When we expect something out of our work, we become selfish. Then we do the work for our benefit. This will incur more karma for us. Even when we are doing some social service, the intention is important. If we do social service to earn a better name for ourselves or receive some recognition, then we have a selfish interest. This is not selfless. When we do social service with the sole purpose of helping others without expecting any return, then we are selfless.

There is a very subtle difference between working for money and working for real service. For example, an entrepreneur sets up a business and works very hard. As long as he is working hard so that his organisation performs better and makes good products or services for the betterment of people in society, directly or indirectly, there is no problem. And in that process definitely, he will make more money and that is all his. But when making money becomes his sole purpose, then his interest becomes selfish. Then he gets attached to the fruits of his action.

Your professional performance will improve due to spiritual practices. With an intuitive mind, you will make more correct decisions in the workplace. As your calmness and ability of self-control improves due to meditation, your work efficiency will improve. You will be less distracted at work. The highs and lows of the material world will not disturb you so much, you will be more even-minded. With the improvement of professional performance, all associated benefits like more money, promotion, or recognition will come to you. That is all yours. The difference is you are not working for them. You are not attached to those material benefits. Tomorrow, if you lose them, it does not affect you. You realize the temporary nature of those material benefits.

Nowadays a lot of people work in technology. Technological development has made our lives much better. Advanced medical service, easy communication, all information at the tip of your finger due to the internet, comfortable life, and luxuries which were even not possible to imagine earlier are all possible due to the development of science and technology. It is the contribution of all those who invented these technologies, developed products, and made life better for mankind. These are all right work.

But then there is also the dark side of technology. People misuse technology to kill people, fight wars, steal money, and so on. The purpose of these people is selfish and they are not contributing to the development of mankind.

Make the world a better place to live. That is expected from all of us. Anything we do to achieve this goal is rightful duty. The world will be a better place if we all become selfless. And through selfless work, we can achieve the supreme goal of knowing God.

Manu: I have a doubt now. Happiness is the goal of our life. But you also said knowing God is our supreme Goal. Is there no conflict?

Papa: Excellent point. I am happy you are thinking deeply about what we are discussing. This will surely help you to live a happy life.

Actually, there is no conflict between these two goals.

Seeking permanent happiness and seeking God are the same.

As we discussed, we cannot get permanent happiness unless we seek God. Nothing on this earth can give us absolute bliss because our true nature is divine. Only by realising our divine nature can we get real happiness. The meaning of real happiness for a self-realised person is knowing God.

Whichever we choose as our goal, the actions are going to be the same. There are only two actions that we need to do. Right work in the right way and dedicated practice of meditation following the right technique under a qualified guru. This is how we can know God and also achieve real happiness.

Manu: One more doubt I have. We seek real happiness for ourselves. Is that not selfish? Is achieving real happiness for ourselves, not a selfish desire.

Papa: It is a difficult question. I am glad that you are asking this.

If a bird kept in a cage wants to become free and fly in the sky, will you call the bird selfish? This is what you are asking. Let me explain to you.

Seeking real happiness, seeking to know our true nature, and seeking to know God are all the same. We just discussed that. When we are in a delusive state and have not realised our true nature, we think we are different from God. We think we are ego. With this ignorance, when we say we seek real happiness for ourselves, it sounds selfish.

But when we are free from delusion and realize our true nature, we know we are the soul. The soul is the image of God. We are divine. After realising that you are divine, you will not say seeking real happiness is selfish. You are not asking anything different from yourself. You are seeking to know your true self. Knowing your true self cannot be selfish.

Strictly speaking, at the time of realising God or achieving the highest state of Samadhi, no desire exists. When we say someone has the desire to know God means God and that someone is two different. Samadhi is union with God or becoming one with God. So, at that point, even that desire to know God will not be there. First, we change our bad desire to good desire, then we transcend our desire to know God and then we become desireless or one with God.

The bird belongs to the open sky. If she wants to go back to the open sky, she cannot be selfish. We belong to the divine world. Our desire to return back to the divine world is not selfish.

Manu: I understand now. But still, I have some apprehension. Is it not a big change from what generally we do?

Papa: It may look like a big change to us, but if you think deeply, it is not.

All the professions that we have now are all rightful duties. Doctors, Engineers, Scientists, Teachers, Entrepreneurs, Farmers, the helpers that you see in public places, Drivers, and Policemen all are working for the service of the people. There is no difference here. People are already doing their rightful duties.

However, the difference is how we look at the work. We need to look at our work selflessly. We need to do our work as a service to mankind, not to fulfil our selfish desires. In fact, this is an expectation now also. The only difference is we expect it from others, but we ourselves don't do it.

When you go to a hospital, you expect the doctor to treat you selflessly. You don't expect the doctor to do something that helps him to make more money. You expect your teacher to teach you so that you can learn better. You don't expect the teacher to teach you in such a way that it is more helpful for her. You say a product is good when it is beneficial for you. You don't expect someone to make a product good for him and sell it to you. You don't want a shopkeeper to sell something to you at a higher price. We even expect a cleaner to do a good cleaning job.

So, we all expect selfless service from others. This is possible only when we all become selfless. As long as we are working to satisfy our ego and build our identity with material achievements, we cannot become selfless. When we can free ourselves from the delusion of ego and know our divine nature, then no material desire can affect us. Then we are free to do selfless service for the betterment of mankind. We become sattvic. Yoga is the path to this freedom.

Performing our rightful duty selflessly and doing regular meditation are linked together. And both are linked with our goal of realising real happiness in life.

This is how we can complete the game of life jigsaw puzzle with an optimal number of puzzle pieces and having the mandatory piece of real happiness. Then we will never feel incomplete in our lives.

We have the free choice to decide whether we play our life puzzle game as per the hidden rule to keep our life simple and feel complete in life or misuse our free choice to make our life more complicated and incomplete. The choice is ours.

Knowledge and the realisation of spirituality are like a compass in our life. When we feel lost in our life journey with many conflicting priorities, they will guide us on the right path. Then we will never say we don't understand life.

I think it is late again today. Tomorrow I will definitely answer your question!!

Manu: I will wait for your answer. Good night.

Papa: Good night.

****

• 7 •

You Are Free

Manu: Today the whole day I was thinking about what we discussed in the last few days. I think I asked you the wrong question. Instead of asking what I should do when I grow up, I should have asked you how I can be happy in life.

Papa: That is wisdom. Now you know what you want in your life.

However, when you think about how to get happiness in life, your question about what you should do when you grow up is still relevant.

The right question that each of us should ask is what we should do in life to be happy.

Remember, we are talking about real happiness, not momentary pleasure. We all know many things that can give us momentary pleasure, but now we have learned what can give us real happiness.

Rightful duty with non-attachment or nishkama karma and dedicated practice of meditation is what is needed to achieve the goal of real happiness. These are the optimal pieces to complete the jigsaw puzzle game of our life. This will keep our life simple and we will get the mandatory happiness. This is the hidden rule of our life.

Now, to answer your question about what you should do in life to be happy, you can take any profession in your life where you have an interest and you get opportunities.

Actually, it does not matter which profession you take. You can be happy in any profession if you follow the hidden rules of life.

Abdul Kalam initially wanted to fly. However, he was not selected for the interview. Later he became a very successful scientist and also the successful president of India.

Everyone knows how simpler life Kalam used to live, but how big were his dreams. He is a role model of simple living and high thinking to all of us. He is an example to all of us of how selfless service to mankind is possible. The following quote from him summarises the influence of spirituality in his life -

"As far as the fact of my religion is concerned, from Rameswaram, I followed my destiny that took me into the world of science and technology. I was always a believer in science, but the spiritual atmosphere of my youth has stayed with me. I well understand different points of view, particularly about God. I have read and assimilated the knowledge contained in different religious texts—from the Koran to the Gita to the Holy Bible. Together they have made me a product of this unique land of ours, a syncretic creation of the best of our diverse traditions." [14]

He was brought up in a religious environment in the pilgrimage town of Rameswaram, the influence of which remained throughout his life. He read and learned the spiritual truths from the great scriptures of different religions. And together that has made him what he is.

It is not important what profession he took, but it is important for us to learn how selflessly he performed his rightful duty.

He understood the hidden rules of life. He did not go behind many material things for happiness, instead, he was satisfied with few possessions and lived a very simple life. We all should learn from his life. Hope I have answered your question now.

Manu: I need to find out what will be my rightful duty. Now I don't know that.

Now I have the opportunity to study and learn more things.

I am not sure what will be my interest in future. Based on my interest and what I study, whatever opportunity I get to do something better for humanity will be my rightful duty.

As you said it could be anything like a doctor, an engineer, a scientist, a teacher, an entrepreneur, or any other profession.

It is not very important what I do, but how I do it is more important.

Papa: Yes. The right work in the right way - this is the code of work we discussed.

Actually, meditation is the key. If you practice meditation correctly for a long time and persevere in it, then most of the other things will happen automatically. It will expand your consciousness and you will manifest your divine qualities.

Gradually you will find yourself very calm, you will see that you are exercising more self-control and the ability to control your anger and other temptations improving, you will find most of your decisions are right and you will start trusting your conscience more. You will become a loving and caring person. You will also find that your priorities in life have changed. You are not thinking more about material aspirations, instead, you are more willing to perform selfless service. You will have very few worries and fears. Even your work performance will be enhanced.

All these changes will gradually manifest in you as you continue to practice meditation. Though it may look like they are happening automatically, now you can understand why they are happening. Your manifested nature is changing from ego to soul. The Kundalini force resting in the coccygeal is moving up the astral spine and your consciousness is moving up the causal spine. Sattva is becoming your dominant guna. As a result of this, you are manifesting the divine qualities, which is your true nature. This is scientific.

Manu: That makes it simpler. If I practice meditation regularly and correctly, other things will happen automatically. That is really nice.

Papa: Yes. That is why I said meditation is the path to happiness.

Manu: I wonder why meditation is not mandatory for all!!

Papa: Spiritual wisdom has been present since ancient times, however, true happiness still eludes most of the common people. Our rational minds often refuse to acknowledge spiritual truths.

I am no exception to that. I realised this only recently when I started thinking seriously about what can bring real fulfillment to me. In spite of being successful in my professional career, I still felt some kind of emptiness within me. I don't think another promotion at my work or buying another house or an expensive car will fill that void within me. I wanted to know what is the source of real happiness. I spent many years exploring this, reading many books about science and psychology, before I found the answer in spirituality.

I realised it when I was already more than fifty years of age. This is too late. One should know this wisdom early in life to get the real benefit of spirituality. That is why I am spending so much time with you now so that you know what is the source of real happiness and how to achieve it.

Throughout our discussion in the last few days, you have learned the facts. Now you don't believe in the myths. We discussed three important myths.

Myth 1: We will be happy if we fulfil our worldly desires. The fact is worldly things can give us only momentary pleasure, not real happiness.

Myth 2: We can understand life with intelligence. The fact is we need intuition to understand life. Only intelligence is not sufficient.

Myth 3: There is no scientific basis for spirituality. The fact is spiritual knowledge is realised scientifically.

You have also learned the five truths of life that existed since time immemorial. Our birth, life, and death are governed by these truths, whether we recognise them or not.

Truth 1: Consciousness is the only reality. Everything else originates from consciousness.

Truth 2: Our physical body functions the way it is functioning now because of the astral and causal body.

Truth 3: Our true nature is soul, but we think we are ego.

Truth 4: We live in an eternal life cycle. Our own work influences this life cycle.

Truth 5: Each one of us is different because of the three gunas. There is a cosmic influence on who we are today.

Spirituality is not only about telling the truth of our existence. Spirituality also teaches us how we should live our lives. We have learned the two important tools that we should use in our day-to-day lives to achieve real happiness.

Tool 1: Meditation.

Tool 2: Nishkama Karma (Right work in the right way).

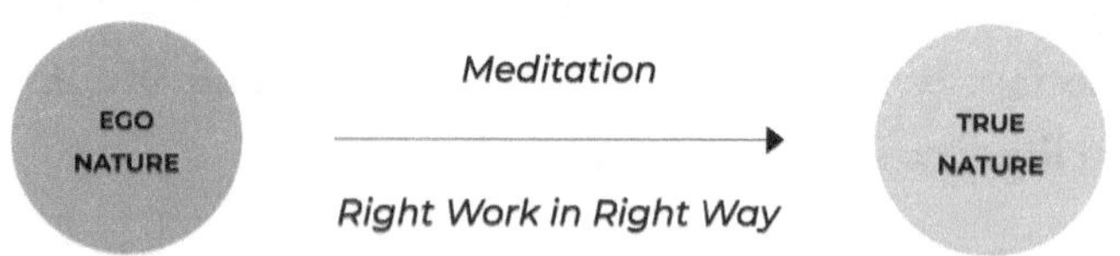

We all understand the role of education in our lives. We don't doubt what we learn in our schools and colleges. Without education, we will remain illiterate. Learning is an integral part of our life. Almost everyone goes to schools and colleges. No one questions why one should study.

In the same way, we need to understand the role of spirituality in our lives and need not doubt spiritual knowledge and practices. Without the knowledge and practice of spirituality, we will remain unhappy in life.

If we want happiness, spirituality should become an integral part of our daily life, the way education is today.

Manu: One last question. Do you think I will be able to realize my true nature and achieve real happiness?

Papa: If you want, you can create another Universe.

You are as powerful as God. Your soul is made of the image of God. Your true nature is divine.

God has given you free choice.

You can decide if you want to realize your true nature and be really happy or remain ignorant and continue to live a delusive life. The choice is yours.

You are pure consciousness. Realise your true nature to be really happy. **You are free.**

Bibliography

1. Kalam, A P J Abdul; Tiwari, Arun. *Transcendence: My Spiritual Experiences with Pramukh Swamiji.* Element India. Kindle Edition.

2. Yogananda, Paramahansa. *God Talks with Arjuna: The Bhagavad Gita: Royal Science of God-Realization.* Yogoda Satsanga Society of India. Kindle Edition.

3. Vivekananda, Swami. *Practical Vedanta.* UNKNOWN. Kindle Edition.

4. Bawra, Brahmrishi Vishvatma. *Samkhya Karika with Gaudapadacarya Bhasya.* Brahmrishi Yoga Publications.

5. Yukteswar, Swami Sri. *The Holy Science.* Yogoda Satsanga Society of India. Kindle Edition.

6. Vivekananda, Swami. *Karma Yoga* (Annotated Edition). Kindle Edition.

7. Vivekananda, Swami. *Jnana Yoga* (Annotated Edition). Kindle Edition.

8. Planck, Max. "*Das Wesen der Materie*" [The Nature of Matter], speech at Florence, Italy (1944)

9. Planck, Max. '*The Observer*', Interview (1931)

10. Vivekananda, Swami. *Raja Yoga,* UNKNOWN. Kindle Edition.

11. Yogananda, Paramahansa. *Autobiography of a Yogi* (Complete Edition). Yogoda Satsanga Society of India. Kindle Edition.

12. Maharshi, Ramana. *The Spiritual Teaching of Ramana Maharshi.* Shambhala. Kindle Edition.

13. Yogananda, Paramahansa. *Man's Eternal Quest: Collected Talks & Essays on Realizing God in Daily Life, Volume I* . Yogoda Satsanga Society of India. Kindle Edition.

14. Kalam, A.P.J. Abdul. *My Journey: Transforming Dreams into Actions.* Rupa Publications Private Limited. Kindle Edition.

15. Yogananda, Paramahansa. *Journey to Self-realization: Collected Talks & Essays on Realizing God in Daily Life.* Yogoda Satsanga Society of India. Kindle Edition.

* * *

www.ingramcontent.com/pod-product-compliance
Lightning Source LLC
Chambersburg PA
CBHW021418260726
48782CB00053B/289

* 9 7 9 8 8 9 1 8 6 8 8 1 6 *